Introduction

As the editor of this second Latino anthology, I have had the opportunity to discuss viewpoints and argue ideas, but, most important I have been able to learn from several very talented and interesting poets and writers.

This project started in January of 1997, with a handful of people signing on to make it a reality, especially Mark Fraire, w.r. rodriguez and Ann Barker. Their insights and support were invaluable at this stage of the project. There were several people who assisted on the pre-production end of the process: Leah Downey, initial typesetting; Phoebe Hefko, Website development; and Teresa Elguézabal and Rubén Medina with the initial screening of submissions to the manuscript. Teresa, along with Daisy Cubias, Nydia Rojas, and Cristina Herrera, made frequent calls to check on the progress of the project and, even though I might not have sounded happy when they asked if it was done yet, I appreciate their encouragement and offers to assist in making the project whole. Angela Villarreal Ratliff, Trino Sánchez, and Sara Morales also lended some needed moral and technical support. Craig Castro pitched in at the end and did excellent proofreading.

Finally, I want to thank Ana Valdés for doing the final layout and Spanish editing and making this literary project come to fruition. Her tireless work made it a success for the entire Latino community in Wisconsin and the Midwest.

We want to thank all the funders of this project:
Lynn Eich and the Dane County Cultural Affairs
Commission, Dean Amhaus and the Wisconsin
Sesquicentennial Fund, and The Puffin Foundation.

We also appreciate the assistance of Vern Visick
and Joy Bailey of the Madison Campus Ministry.

Special thanks to the staff at Lakeview Library
under the leadership of Katie Scharf and Walter
Sava of the United Community Center for
sponsoring pre-production reading. Gracias as well
to the Latino Writers Group organized by Teresa
Elguézabal, Nydia Rojas, and Rubén Medina.

I also want to thank the Board of Directors and staff
of Omega School. They have listened to my
struggles with this project and have been very
understanding.

This has been a very difficult year for me. Losing
my mother Micaela Mireles this summer has been
one of the most significant losses in my life. I was
in the hospital room moments before she died and
saw firsthand how quickly life and death are
interconnected. I dedicate this book to her memory.
Her funeral was a celebration of old friends from
my old neighborhood and new friends coming
together as a testament to her presence and
influence on their lives during her short time on this
earth. I miss her so much. I didn't realize it until

one of my board members, Betsy Draine, asked how I was doing and let it be known that it was ok to mourn for awhile.

Thanking your immediate family for their support is a time-honored tradition. While I have read poetry to several of my children's school classes, it is not always clear to them that I have a real job and that I write poetry sometimes. My last literary effort occurred when my oldest child, Diego was three years old; Diego Jesus is now 12 and in middle school. I want to thank my other children along with Diego for their energy, vision and honesty. Lorena Pilar, Sergio Andres, and Javier Oscar have made me a better poet and father and person. My wife Clara has been my most ardent supporter, patient observer, and inspiration. Through it all, she demonstrates a commitment to show me all facets of her love and her search for excellence in myself and my family. I have always admired this trait. Gracias por todo. Thanks for everything....

Oscar Mireles September 1999

Table of Contents

Cultural Identity

Death and Things Worse

Sisterhood

Mothers and Fathers

Ideology and Action

Elvis Presley Was Chicano

In the latest edition
of the National Inquirer
it was revealed that

Elvis Presley
Yes… the legendary Elvis
was a Chicano

Fans were outraged,
critics cite his heritage
as an important influence
I was stunned!
Can you believe it?

I didn't really at first
but then I remembered
his jet black hair
you know with the little curl in the front
sort of reminded me of my cousin Chuy

and Elvis always wore
either those tight black pants
like the ones on West Side Story
or a baggy pin-striped Zoot Suit
Pachuco style
with a pair of
blue suede shoes to match

Then I figured no, it couldn't be
so I traced his story
back to his home town

a little pueblo outside Tupelo
a son of migrant parents
looking for a way out
of rural poverty

Let's see… Elvis joined the Army
maybe he enlisted
with a group of his buddies
because a lot of Chicanos have fought
in many of the wars for this country,
they never made a movie about it,
but they fought valiantly anyway

Elvis was a loner, yet he was a hero
and I read somewhere that Chicanos
have won more military
Silver Stars and Purple Hearts
than any other ethnic group
maybe he was…
I wasn't convinced yet

Elvis was a dancer, a ladies man
and always won the girl that hated him
in the beginning of the movie
he had to be a Latin lover or something
even Valentino and Sinatra
had a little Italian in them

Elvis played guitar
like my uncle Carlos
always hitting the same four notes
over and over again

But, now I think I've figured it out
it was probably Colonel Parker's idea
to change his cultural identity
since it was just after the war
and the Zoot Suit riots

It wasn't time for a Chicano superstar
to be pelvising around on the Ed Sullivan show
especially after church

I think it was just a hoax
to convince more people
to buy that newspaper
if Elvis really was a Chicano
he wouldn't have settled
to die alone
in an empty mansion

with no familia around
who cared enough
to cry

Oscar Mireles

WHATCHOO CALL ME?

Hi, my name's Sarah Teniente. Yes, that's *Sarah* with an H. Well, the question of my identity, that's what you asked me about. Right? The question of my identity started before I was even born. Well, actually the day I was born.

I was born in Berlin, Wisconsin in 1971. I hear it's called New Berlin nowadays. In those days, according to my father, who loves to tell stories about his kids, we were the only Mexican family in the whole town. I was the last one born in the old hospital. Right after I was born they moved me into the new hospital. Then, when it came time to sign the birth certificate, my dad noticed they wrote my name Sarah, with an H instead of Sara without an H, the way it's written in Spanish.

"That stubborn old nurse! She told me that I wasn't spelling it right. She said it's spelled S-A-R-A-H. !Que pendeja! She was so stubborn, even more than me! Can you imagine? Well, she never changed it and that's why you ended up Sarah, with an H."

For many years I wrote my name S-A-R-A, for my dad and in protest to the injustice of the stubborn old nurse. But the day came when I had to sign *official papers*. They said I had to write my name the way it appeared on my birth certificate. To change it I would have to go to court and publish it in the newspapers. It would cost time and money ... just to take one letter, that H, from my name.

For me it was the difference between a Mexican identity and an American one. But, by the time they said it would cost money, my parents, who don't like to spend money *de oquís* said:

"Leave it alone, it isn't worth it anymore."
"But..."
"¡Ya Aplácate!"

After that, I didn't bring it up anymore. I started to write SARAH with an H. Sarah, Sarah Teniente, until I forgot that I didn't like it.

El quintergarden: I showed up the first day of school in braids and a dress. I was the only little girl in a dress, and the only Mexican. My English wasn't that great, but I was ready to learn everything they were going to teach me. Before I even went to school my dad bought me a school desk at a garage sale. Me and my older sister María Elena used to play school. She was a tough teacher. By the time I got to kindergarten I knew how to spell my name in cursive. But my "real" teacher wouldn't let me write my name that way. I didn't like her much. Fortunately, I had another teacher, Miss González, who taught my bilingual class. I thought she was the most beautiful woman in the world. After my mom. Anyways, it was great to be able to go to her class and get away from the kids who pulled my braids.

One day while I was walking down the long hallway to Miss González's class I saw a little boy sitting outside the principal's office. He was older than me, I guessed he was probably 7 or 8 years old.

He was a little blond kid with really pale skin. I noticed he had been watching me for a while and when I got closer he said something, but I didn't understand:

" ¿Qué? ... I mean, what did you say?"

"Spic!"

"Espeak? Jes, I espeak englisch.

"NO! I called you a spic! Dummy, you're just a dumb taco-bender"

"Tacos?" I said. "I don't know how to make tacos, I'm too little."

The guerito made a weird face then turned away from me. I was thoroughly confused. By the time I got to my bilingual class I had forgotten about it. It wasn't until I got home that I remembered. I decided to ask my mom how people could tell whether or not you could make tacos just by looking at you. My mom was in the kitchen having a cup of coffee with my tía Teresa.

"Soco, *did you see* how that loca de Tencha was dressed? With that tight *skirt* up to here? Her nalgas were practically hanging out for everybody to see!" my tía said.

"¡Ay Teresa!" my mom said laughing. "¡Que escandalosa eres!"

Mamí..." I said trying to interrupt. 'I think she's up to something with the *jefe*," my tía continued. "Ma ... Mamí ... ma..." I kept trying to interrupt. "Sí, sí, my mom said. "Those are the rumors at work."

"Ma ... Mamí, " I said a little louder while pulling on her sleeve. "Ma..." "¿Qué quieres?" my mom yelled at me. "Can't you see I'm talking to your tía?"
I stood there shocked with my mouth hanging open.
"Esperando que me entraba las moscas, like my dad would always say - waiting for the flies to enter my mouth. It took me a couple of seconds to remember what I was going to ask her.

"How can you tell if somebody knows how to make tacos?"
"¿Qué?" my mom said.
While I told what happened to me at school, my brother had come to the table to eat a sandwich.

"Teresa," my mom asked my tía. "Do you know what it means to say taco-bender?"

"It's like saying spic," my twelve-year-old brother said.
"Spic?" my mother and my tía said at the same time.
"Oh yeah," I said. "He said that to me too."

"You guys don't know nothing," my brother told them. "Saying spic is like calling a black person a Nigger."

"Javier!" My mom scolded. "I don't want to hear you use that word!"

"But ma," my brother said. "It's true."

7

I looked at my mother. "Is it bad to say Nigger?"

"YES! I never want to hear you use that word!"

She gasped. I stood there staring at my mother. I was really super confused after that. My mom got nervous and looked at my tía for support but she was reading a magazine. My mother turned to face me.

"Mija, if that boy says something to you again ... tell him he doesn't know what he's talking about."

"Okay ma," I said.

I didn't understand why they reacted that way, but I started to feel real bad. I decided to go to my room where I laid on my bed and stared at the ceiling. *What a dummy,* I thought to myself, *no wonder that kid was making faces at me. But why? I didn't do nothing to him. I don't even know him.* Just then my brother came into my room and sat on my bed. I sat up to sit next to him. He started to talk to me, but he never looked at me. He looked real serious.

"Sara, tomorrow I'll take you to school."
"Okay."
"When we get to school show me the boy that said that stuff to you today."
"Okay."
'But don't say anything to mom, okay?"
"Uh-huh," I said smiling.
"Okay, good," he said and with that he left my room.

8

The next day I proudly strolled into school with my brother at my side. It wasn't long before I saw the guerrito and marched up to where he was.

"That's him," I said pointing directly at him.

I don't know what my brother said to him, but that kid never said anything to me ever again. In fact, he never even looked at me if he could help it. After that, nobody who knew that I was a TENIENTE, or knew my brother and my cousins ever messed with me again.

Sarah Teniente

Weeh Con Sohn*!*

Please do not ask me whether I speak Mexican.
Mexican is not a language . It is a culture, a people
from the country of Mexico. When we first arrived
in Wisconsin (pronounced "Weeh-con-sohn"), we
were wondering if we looked Mexican. Locals
politely would make remarks like "let me tell you
where to get the best burrito in town," or "My
husband and I went to Cancún for a second
honeymoon-and the people were so friendly!"

¡Ay ya yai! we thought. They all think we're from
Mexico! Then we discovered that the majority of
the Hispanic culture represented here in this area are
people from Mexico or of Mexican ancestry.
Soooo…, we thought, it is time to say a little about
who we are as Hispanics.

The word comes somewhere from the island of
Hispanola-present-day Dominican Republic and
Haiti. This was where Christopher Columbus first
landed (it is believed). In fact, presently Cristóbal
Colón (in Spanish) is actually buried on that island.
Well anyhow, the term Hispano was used to
identify people who came from that island. Later as
things got complicated and empires fought for
territory, the term Hispano came to mean anyone
who shared in a common heritage. That is, anyone
born in the New World who was the product of the
conquest. This is very politely said. Some would
rather say that those who were the result of the rape
of the native peoples of the Americas, and the
displaced Africans taken as slaves, were now called

all together Hispanos or Hispanics. Now you may understand why Hispanics hardly use the Discovery credit card-it brings bad memories.

You know I like that word "discovery." "The Discovery of the Americas." Let me share a Contemporary Hispanic view of this epic-sounding term. Let's say I walk into your house and I see your 32" Zenith TV. And I stand in the middle of your living room or wherever you have your TV and declare (with one arm outstretched) "I have *discovered* your TV." "I will take it to my house." You get mad and throw your Bucky Badger ashtray at me. I duck, pull out my sword, cut your head off, rape your wife, and sell your kids. This is the view of the *Discoveree!*

Because of this history we have taken pride in who we have become through our independence from the conquerors or discoverers. While we all share a common heritage and similar past, our histories are all unique and different. Just by traveling through our countries you will notice that while we all speak a common language we look very different. Some may have dominant native or indigenous features, while others more of a European look, and still others with African features. We are mulatto and mestizo, black and white-and yes, all Hispanic. But our pride and the key to who we are comes in our differences.

If you ask a guy from Buenos Aires what he is, he'll tell you that he is an argentino. If you ask him if he's Hispanic, he'll probably say no-I'm an Argentine! If you ask a woman from Peru if she's

Hispanic, she'll probably say no, she'll say "¡Yo soy peruana! (I am Peruvian)." If you persist in asking what they are they'll say that they are South Americans or Latin Americans at best. Something really weird happens when we travel to the North American continent. We become Hispanics. Its like cultural jet lag. We lose our nationality, our culture, our history, and yes sometimes our pride because we are grouped together as this non-descript bland thing called Hispanic. Ah yes, I believe the politically correct term is now "Latino". I guess because it's a Spanish word and it carries more authenticity or something.

Oh, also another thing happens when we go north: we become a minority. This is tough to deal with. Talk about an identity crisis. That is like if I were to say all Australians, Britons, Americans (United States), Irish, and Canadians living in Cuba were Texans. I would make this claim because I met a Texan family who moved to Cuba and they spoke English. Furthermore I would assume that peoples of all these countries loved chili, wore cowboy hats, and are football fans. Cheez, (or rather cheese head) that is as bad as confusing a Packer fan for a Chicago Bears fan-woooo, don't go there!

Now to further confuse you. There is a difference between, say, a Venezuelan who was born in Venezuela and immigrated to the U.S. and one who was born, educated, and has been living here all his life. The latter has more in common with a rhubarb-eating midwesterner than he does with someone his age living in Caracas. Now when both of these are standing at the checkout at the Pick N

Save in McFarland, they are both Hispanics. Now you figure it out! The "Hispanic" who was born here thinks of himself as an American, just like any other one born and living in the U.S.A. But not only is he Hispanic, he also is a minority-mainly because of his looks and because his surname is either Hernández or Pérez or something in Spanish. What a mess!

I hope I have been somewhat helpful, and not totally confusing. Anyway, next time you see one of us in Wisconsin, take a moment and ask us about our countries of origin, our backgrounds, and our foods. We'll be more than happy to share with you our culture and traditions. Perhaps the more we learn about one another the more we can appreciate the beauty of humanity expressed in many languages and styles. Oh, and by the way, while I'm not Mexican, I love their salsa!

Ed Gómez

The Color Brown

Brown
is but a color
a color that has many setbacks
Brown
is but a color
that is a synonym of
discrimination and hate
Brown
is but a color
that is to some
a race with no goals, love, or
respect
Brown
is but a color
a color that is to me
love, hope, and self-respect
Brown
is but a color
that IS me
because I AM brown, and
Brown
is but a color

Cassandra Morales-Saenz

Where are you from?

Otra vez,
ayer alguien me preguntaba,
"Where are you from?"

Cuando me preguntan una vez, está bien.
No me enfado si aceptan mi respuesta
de que soy de Madison.

Pero,
A veces esperan una respuesta exótica,
y se molestan cuando no lo es.
A veces esperan oír el nombre de algún lugar
remoto y desconocido,
algo como
Jocotepec, Tuxcueca o Tizapán el Alto.

No satisfechos,
vuelven a su pregunta.

"Really, where are you from?"
Soy de Madison.

"But your name is different. Where is it from?"
¡Insisten machacando la paciencia!

Ya medio enfadado,
medio con ganas de jugar con ellos, respondo:
¿Por qué?

"It is very long and hard to say."
Ah! I see. ¿De veras?

¡Idiotas!

Pienso en silencio.

Sé lo qué buscan con sus preguntas, pero insisto
en fastidiarlos.
Si quieren respuesta,
que les cueste.
Soy de Modesto.
"Where is that, in Mexico?"
No, en California.
"But you have an accent."
Y Ud. también. *"Where are you from?"*
"I am from here."
¡Pues yo también!
¿Por qué, coño, no quiere Ud. aceptar
que yo también soy de aquí?
¿Acaso no sabía que
también hay latinos en Wisconsin?

Alfonso Zepeda-Capistrán

The Day I Threw Thoreau Off the Roof

was three days after a riot, was two days after our
    mayor
toured the property damage, was a day after the
    radio told
me I lived in a slum, was my first day off work in
    months.
the day I threw thoreau off the roof, was a hot day
    which
melted the tar, was another day of the mosquitoes
    which bred
in the backwater of the sewer our city would never
    fix and bit
anything that could still bleed. the day I threw
    thoreau
off the roof, was the angry day I refused to do my
    homework,
was the happy day I watched yellow pages flutter
    down the air shaft
like poisoned pigeons. the day I threw thoreau off
    the roof,
was not up to civil disobedience, was just sick of
    reading
about those damn beans.

w r rodriguez

Self Portrait

My urns are full of cultural treasures,
my heart beats with the rhythm of African drums,
my soul is nourished by the rays of the sun, the
    Incan God...
My mind travels with the Spanish vessels in the
    Indian Ocean.

My life is a field where the seeds of many cultures
    have been planted,

The morning dew of the times, nurturing their
    growth, kissing their petals.

I am rich, by history and tradition. By the grace of
    GOD
I've walked the many roads, followed my ancestors
    and as I stand half way into my journey,
I reach for my urns, full of strength, of love and
    history
and steady as a rock, move towards the future.

Gladis Benavides

Oscurito Spick

y entonces [Mutezuma] alzó las vestiduras y me
mostró el cuerpo diciendo: "A mí véisme aquí que
soy de carne y hueso como vos y como cada uno, y
que soy mortal y palpable".
Segunda carta de relación, Hernán Cortés

El contrayente
trabalenguas
multiétnico
que me rodea

me escupe
que
soy
    alienado
        alien
    sanguijuela
        welfareizado
    el más mojado
        de los mojados
    simpatizante
        feminazi
    cabrón
        comunistoide
    pendejo
        fascistoide
    oscurito
        spick
    envergado
        cerebro
    libre

pensador

egocéntrico

macho

vendido

agringado

insensible

cerdo

ciudadano

colombogringo

objetificador

femenino

chofereado

sodomizador

demonio

gweilou

aculturado

bárbaro

transculturador

seudo

intelectualoide

perdido

poetizador

retro

racista

mestizante

mierda

chibcha

sensitive

new age guy

práctico

esteta

postmoderno

    conservador

iconoclasta

    étnico

venenoso

    profesor

aminorada

    minoría

descristianizado

    cristiano

pussy-whipped

    opresor

desasimilado

    inmigrante

irreverente

    respetuoso

montado

    montador

cuestionante

    voz

desmadrado

    padre

borderizado

    intercultural

prostituido

    prostituyente

    por años
    afónico
    he respondido
    soy humano

Rino Avellaneda

I look in the mirror

I look in the mirror
for the names
you have called me
they escape me
every one

accusations of color
language
headlines
are frozen snapshots
in a moving picture

I wait between frames
dancing
thinking

politically correct hands
show me negatives
of the same pictures
anxious for the names
they can never claim
but wish to inherit
through guilt
through association

Look! I say
in the boxes
underneath beds
stacked in closets

can these places hold
the names that are written
in strands of hair
trace the geography
under your fingernails
translate the voice
behind your eyes

you can hear them
names-places-voices
growing out of the Earth
ask your feet
they know

if you look for your face
in albums and embassies
certificates and tribal rolls
you will find
what can only be lost
just as easily

what has brought you here is good
trust the wisdom of uncertainty
it keeps you honest
attentive
reverent

if you omit
one place
one name
one idea
one molecule

then you splinter truth
into fragments and fractions
and your reflection
will be full of shadows
your story incomplete

who are you and
where do you come from

there may be a word for it
but it won't fit
on the dotted line
don't settle for pat definitions
the unsettling is your destiny

continents shift
memories drift
and spores move across galaxies

don't be lulled into forgetfulness
by a card-carrying culture

remember who you are
...all of it

Cristina Herrera

PAYASO

I am not your clown!
No I'm NOT your clown!
I am definitely not your clown!
NO, I don't wear oversized shoes!
NO, I don't wear baggy trousers
with tablecloth patches!
NO, I don't wear polka-dotted bow-ties,
long funny-looking ties, wide ties
or ties that reach down to my knees.
NO, I don't wear make-up!
NO, I don't have a red nose!
NO, I don't have big ears!
NO, I don't have sad eyes!
NO, I don't have red and blue hair!
I'm not employed by Barnum & Bailey.
I haven't been to a circus in years.
NO, that is not sawdust on my shoes.
NO, I don't run around horny ...
I mean tweeting my horn!
How many times must I tell you
I am NOT a clown and
No, I don't spend my life
making other people laugh. But ...

if you want to clown around call me
on the telephone: 1 800 C H I-C A N O!

Trinidad Sánchez, Jr.

25

LA-DF

Los que andan
por aquí y por allá
como peces en río revuelto
arrastrados por la corriente:
Wilshire Boulevard, Brooklyn, Alvarado,
y en un paso a desnivel,
Calzada Nonoalco, Bucareli, Fray Servando,
y parecen olvidados
hacia qué mar se dirigen.

Los que llevan
a otra ciudad
bajo la piel
y parecen ignorar
que el país no termina
en el hachazo,
las tardes de lluvia,
el amor de secundaria,
el dinero de cada mes,
las cartas de los amigos
y la tormenta
que se avecina.

Los que tienen
el pulso de ave
y la respiración
de continente
y parecen atrapados

en un silencio de piedras
porque en cada respiración
y cada paso
ya no hay Tierra Firme.

Esos
somos nosotros:
los que vivimos el hachazo
y el paso a desnivel.

Rubén Medina

Self Portrait

La ví. I saw her.
La mujer de la selva.
The woman of the jungle.
Su pelo mojado escurriendo por su rostro.
I saw her eyes, dark panther eyes,
    watching life from the tree.
¡La ví corriendo! I saw her running!
Running through the jungle hunting nothing at all.
¡Ella grita!
She screams!
She roars. She thrushes her flesh body to memories
    that
denied her love. La ví. La ví razguñando los ojos,
    del hombre de los ojos azules.
I saw her scratching the eyes of a man with blue
    eyes.
¡El esta ciego!
He is blind!
Ella se sonríe con su boca de gata.
She smiles with her cat mouth.
He won't remember.
El no se acuerda.
I saw her!
¡La ví!
La ví sentada desnuda enfrente del espejo.
I saw her naked in front of the mirror.
¡Soy yo!   It's me!
¡Soy yo.!

Margarita Dumit

The Cockfight Bust

police barricade the entire street
squad cars, detective cars, a police bus
spectators everywhere
and down the police-lined path
like a Broadway opening in an old movie
prisoners are herded to meat-market justice
booked and sentenced
to live their lives in anonymous apartments
to fatten and die in the Bronx
but judicious wheels turn slowly
it takes a very long restless time
for two patrol wagons to return and reload
return and reload again and again
everyone gets bored amid all the excitement
so cops run round the block
to roundup strays
escaping through canyons of basements
and catch no one to the crowd's delight
while I count seventy-eight men and women
with blankets and picnic baskets
children and babies
parading out to our applause
they wave and cheer back in temporary fame
everyone is happy as when the circus comes
to the Puerto Rico theater if not happier
because we are all on the stage
of a great dramatic irony
and know from the corners of our eyes
that just down the street el lobo sweeps
the sidewalk he don't know nothing
he's just the janitor here

but damn those are his best fighters
hauled off in the unmarked car
while the bull in charge stands
proud as the cock of the walk
but tomorrow at dawn
roosters again will crow
will they betray him he wonders
and who got the money

w r rodriguez

CHILDREN OF THE ANCIENTS

we are children of the ancients
what flows through our veins is
memory

trust what you know
listen to all you remember
the past walks beside us
we must move forward together

we are children of the ancients
memory is an intricate web
invisible threads connect us
to one another

the waters flow over the face
of this place
and they are inhabited
the trees translate and join
with branches above and below
the stones are living records
taking everything down

we are children of the ancients
approaching our rite of passage
dreaming of what might be

capacities lie dormant in our DNA
we don't understand 9O percent
of our flowering brains
and label the clues
metaphysics

do caterpillars grasp the significance
when they hear the beat of a wing and
see a splash of color fly by

we are children of the ancients
truth falls like rain all around us
feel water caress on its way to the ground

Cristina Herrera

Before Horace Greeley

When Italy was basking in its Renaissance
Spain went west over the ocean.
Before the British colonials,
Before the Irish and Germans, Hungarians, Danish
And the rest, Spain and some of her kin went west.

Small islands and a large continent were found
By the explorers and were soon overtaken
Like unattended picnic food.

Commerce, religion, and politics
Did what their natures deemed best,
They ate the landscape and the culture
of the ancients living there.

Here I sit a descendant of the conquerors and the
conquered,
Spitting out useless observations on a morning
filled
With useless observations.
Looking eastward,
Looking westward,
Restless ever restless.

Pedro Villarreal

Ritos

"*Mon esprit, comme mes vertèbres,*
Invoque ardemment le repos;
Le coeur plein de songes funèbres,

Je vais me coucher sur le dos
Et me rouler dans vos rideaux,
O rafraîchissantes ténèbres!"

"La fin de la journée," Charles Baudelaire

Alboreaba su vida, cuando descubrió la niña el secreto de la mágica poción. Sucedió un día cualquiera, en que habiéndose adentrado en el bosque junto con las demás niñas de la comunidad tribal se pusieron a jugar al escondido. Tras largas y deleitosas horas de alegre correteo, por entre la arboleda, se sintieron aguijoneadas por el húmedo calor de la tarde y por el exceso de actividad física. Y fue entonces que se dirigieron a la cascada para darse una refrescante zambullida. Entre brincos y saltos, muy pronto, hubieron de llegar a su destino.

Una vez allí, se desnudaron con premura y, entre entusiastas gritos, lanzaron a los transparentes brazos del acuoso cuerpo la naciente sensualidad de sus incipientes formas. Cual vivaces pececillos nadaron hasta cansarse de atrapar, por sus palancas, a los langostinos guarecidos en el fondo de la poza, formada por la caída del agua. Entonces probaron el dulce abandono de la calmante sensación de las agujillas del chorro, incrustándoseles en la piel de las espaldas.

Pero... para Ondina, a diferencia del grupo de núbiles princesas con las que conformaba el virginal clan de próximas casaderas, resultó ser esta una singular experiencia... Sentía que el divino líquido le confería un poder muy especial... la facultad de saberse una con la universal sinfonía de la vida. Era como si, de pronto, un chubasco de estrellas se le hubiera metido en la sangre, haciéndosela circular con el calor de su luz ahora fulgente en su mirada.

Y quiso saborear la niña, las ambrósicas promesas del hídrico desbordamiento en todos y cada uno de los rincones de su broncíneo cuerpo. De manera que acostada sobre la comprimida dureza de una enorme piedra, batió las mariposas de las pestañas con fascinación para que pudieran seguir la vertical trayectoria del incoloro bálsamo hacia la turgencia de sus carnes temblorosas. Una breve turbación de los sentidos la sacudió al sentir la sutil, pero vehemente lamida de sus morenos y diminutos pezones por el agua. De inmediato se le irguieron, impeliéndola a palpar con asombro su gomosa dureza. Y así lo hizo, experimentando, para su sorpresa, el mismo vahído de antes, pero con mayor intensidad. Los huesos pélvicos se le arquearon en una involuntaria contracción y afuera todo dejó de existir. Mas fue arrancada de sus placenteros devaneos por la algarabía formada por sus compañeras de juego, dadas ahora en jugar a la pelota con una esfera de raíces. A viva voz la llamaban para que se uniera a su alborozo. Así que se levantó lentamente y con lánguido mirar revisó su entorno. No comprendía, en absoluto, lo que acababa de sucederle, ni mucho menos la corporal metamorfosis a la que estaba concurriendo, pero lo cierto era que contaba con todo lo que podía necesitar... doce años y el novel descubrimiento de su mágica poción. Y era esta una inexcusable verdad que, no con poco regocijo, habría de descubrir dentro de poco. Pero por lo pronto se prometió volver al día siguiente, pues quería, sin saber por qué, volver a probar el dulce extravío provocado por la magia del brebaje adentrándosele por los poros.

Era muy de mañana cuando Ondina tomó la ruta hacia la cascada. La guiaba la impaciencia nacida de la mera necesidad de recuperar la fluctuante sensación de hormigueo, que había amenazado transportarla al olvido la víspera a no ser por el griterío de sus amiguitas. Alelada contempló la bajada del agua, en tanto se desvestía presurosa. Se estremeció con fuerza y se le puso la carne de gallina al sentir la helada de la brisa, producida por el incesante despeñamiento del ácueo cuerpo contra las rocas. Ondina respiró complacida y elevando los brazos al cielo, en íntima ovación ante la imponente belleza del paisaje, comenzó a girar sobre sus talones en el pasto mojado. Dando jocundos saltitos, se dirigió justo hasta la roca que le sirviera de lecho el día anterior. Con felino desenfado se tendió a lo largo de su metálica corporeidad. Los placenteros augurios de la primera vez no se hicieron esperar. De modo que presa por el férvido entusiasmo del día anterior, se aprestó a recuperar los fantásticos efectos de la límpida pócima...

Fue así que incitada por la milenaria fuerza de su instintual curiosidad, Ondina probó regar el tierno botón, que resguardaba el venusino secreto de la flor de su pubes... Una violenta agitación de los sentidos le perturbó vivamente el ánimo y la mantuvo convulsa, exaltada y del todo estimulada ante el descubrimiento de la vital propiedad de su genital gruta y atrapada en un espasmódico ciclo de encogimiento y dilatación de sus músculos enardecidos.

En lo sucesivo, Ondina no habría de ausentarse a una sola de sus citas con la líquida fuga de ensueños. De solo anticipar cada nuevo encuentro, experimentaba una trémula y deliciosa sacudida del vientre bajo y unas ansias incontenibles de recobrar el cálido y ondulante cosquilleo, que la hacía sentirse como derritiéndose por dentro. Ahora estaba muy consciente de la potencial sensualidad de cuanto la rodeaba. Así, disfrutaba enormemente del ligero roce de la inquieta hierba en la piel de los tobillos; de la tímida caricia, prodigada como a hurto, por los lacios mechones de su cabello bailoteándole sobre el cuello, los hombros y la espalda o de ineludibles y furtivos paseos, a solas y desnuda, por entre el húmedo frescor de frondosas avenidas de naranjo. Talmente, se sucedían sus días en una suerte de genesíaco estado de original desembarazo. Ciertamente, la maravillosa poción estaba obrando prodigios en Ondina, pues, de pura complacencia, se le había embellecido la expresión.

Imposible dar cuenta cabal de los bonancibles y abundantes dones concedidos a Ondina por el deífico fluído. Empero, entre los alcanzados, Ondina estimaba inapreciables la posibilidad de dichoso olvido, de reconfortante laxitud de los sentidos y de las extremidades y de poder satisfacer los reclamos de la vital pulsión de sus más recónditos anhelos y necesidades. De tal modo, disfrutaba, como nunca, de toda actividad motivada por el febril impulso de conservación de su existencia, que latía dentro de sí. Invariablemente la preparación medicinal le despertaba las ganas de comer. Entonces devoraba con sensual glotonería pulpas almibaradas y carnosas hasta dejarlas en el hueso, a la vez que por las muñecas se le escurría el azucarado néctar que chupaba con fruición. También tenía la propiedad de restaurarle el sueño su poción. Así, la mayoría de las veces, tras saciarse, echaba reparadoras siestas de las que despertaba con aire tardo e indolente.

Cierta noche, mientras revolvía su insomnio, a causa del calor y los mosquitos, sobre el grueso tejido de esparto de su improvisado lecho de estera, Ondina se resolvió por su poción. Ello dado que estaba cierta de que sería lo único que la devolvería al feliz estado de suspensión de la conciencia. En la rústica vivienda, hecha con adobes y cubierta con cañas a dos aguas, muy vertientes, todos, excepto Ondina, participaban de una letárgica disposición de los sentidos. Así que ella se desplazó con sigilo del lecho con tal de no despertarlos y fue entonces que, una vez atravesado el umbral de su morada, emprendió una loca carrera en dirección a la cascada.

Sin tardanzas se liberó de sus toscas vestiduras de sayal y dominada por la venérea apetencia, que aún no reconocía como tal, se fue diluyendo en la plateada lámina de metal de las aguas en quietud. Iba en busca de su poción... Tendida sobre el dorso, en la misma roca grande y elevada de tantos otros momentos, Ondina se aprestó a la espera...

Entre tanto, en la campestre casilla, la madre de Ondina, prevenida de su ausencia y muy preocupada por ello, se disponía a iniciar su búsqueda...

En posición supina, en la misma roca de otrora, y transfigurada por las luminíferas y étereas ondulaciones del plenilunio, la encontraría finalmente. Así, habría de ocultar entre el denso follaje sus ancestrales culpa y vergüenza y, vacilante entre la fascinación y el espanto, se concentraría en observar a su hija con toda atención.

De tal manera, una serie de inconexas y desgastadas imágenes acudirían, como en tropel, al recuerdo para atormentarla... Entonces sepultaría bajo sus manos los ojos resquebrajados, en el vano intento de anublar su sufrimiento. Pero ni aún así, lograría aplacar la estrepitosa violencia del algente y arrollador alud de tristes memorias. Ovillada sobre la dura superficie de la tierra, la madre de Ondina parecía no más que un confuso montoncito de soledad y angustia. Después sería arrebatada por una suerte de preternatural agitación, al rememorar la implacabilidad del pétreo filo amputando la eréctil propiedad del carnoso cuerpecillo. De modo que al espanto cedería el inicial asomo de fascinación y, a la postre, primaría en ella el pavoroso estado de absoluta consternación del espíritu, que estaba ocasionándole grandes opresión y molestia.

Inadvertida por Ondina, se escurriría con todo sigilo en medio de la arborada. E instigada por la urgencia de su tenaz resolución llegaría a su casa con gran prontitud. Y habida cuenta de la escena de minutos antes, reclinaría su insomnio a la espera de que diera la primera hora de la mañana. Y llegada la ocasión, se dispondría a relatar a su esposo lo acontecido con lujo de detalles. De esta manera, advertirían la apremiante necesidad de dar sacro origen a un evento de especial importancia... el tránsito de Ondina de la niñez a la pubertad. Tocaba pautar, pues, el tiempo y lugar en que el remanente masculino en Ondina sería removido. De suerte que pudiera dar plena expresión a su femineidad.

Era la hora justa en que el sol se halla en oposición al más alto punto de su elevación sobre el horizonte. En la pequeña localidad tribal se efectuaban los sencillos preparativos diligentemente. Ondina, por su parte, observaba con atolondramiento los incesantes movimientos alrededor suyo sin comprender realmente nada o muy poco. Así que con excesiva viveza y escasa reflexión se entretenía en repasar las aúreas cuentecillas y los vítreos canutillos del hermoso abalorio, que le fuera colocado alrededor del cuello por su madre. El vivo y efímero resplandor, despedido por la bella labor, le recordó de súbito su cristalina poción mágica y, como siempre, no pudo eludir el tibio y delicioso haloncillo del fibroso conducto de su recinto pubiano.

Un basto vestido de níveo algodón fue colocado sobre el bronceado cuerpo de Ondina; haciéndola lucir como una virgen vestal, doncella casta entre todas las castas y consagrada al culto de su deidad. Sin embargo, muy pronto, Ondina sería arrancada de su habitual contentura cuando, sin miramientos, fuera tumbada en el suelo y allí retenida por un cortejo de escuálidas comadronas.

Así, a la vez que el grupo de mujeres la sujetaba con férrea firmeza por los antebrazos, los muslos y las convulsas piernas, con el fin de mantenérselas abiertas de par en par, la jefa del tribal acompañamiento de parteras procedió con presteza... Auxiliada por un afilado trozo de vidrio, procedió a cortar de modo limpio, definitivo y a sangre fría la base del tronco y el glande del carnoso y eréctil cuerpecillo y los suaves, elásticos y rizados labios a su alrededor. Luego raspó, con un instrumento oxidado, áspero y cortante, los dos lados restantes del vulvar sangrante antro hasta dejarlos en la carne viva y los cosió apretadamente hasta bloquear, por completo, la tremante y descarnada abertura.

A Ondina, la extraordinaria violencia de un sordo dolor la traspasó justo desde el primer funesto corte. Cual tirantes cuerdas, los nervios le vibraron en un patético desacorde, en una rota y desvariada melodía de desesperación. Fueron las disonantes notas de sus destemplados gritos, las que precedieron al total desconcierto de su corporeidad y a la inminente postración de sus fuerzas vitales.

Mientras tanto, el revejido grupo de acompañantas cantaba sin tregua: "Vamos Ondina, ninfa de las aguas, ya eres toda una mujer. En novia te has convertido. Acercadle un pene, pues para la cópula está dispuesta". Con los cánticos y la baraúnda buscaban sofocar los gritos proferidos por la delirante Ondina.

Finalmente, Ondina colapsó... La anhelosa respiración que mostrara desde los inicios de la operación le cambió, de pronto, en un estertoroso quejido, ronco silbido propio de los agonizantes. Después se apoderó de ella un mórbido sopor y terminó por sumirse en un comatoso sueño del que ya no despertaría jamás.

Y del cuenco de disecada higuera, estratégicamente colocado bajo las tremulantes y broncíneas nalgas, se desbordó lentamente el sanguíneo humor y juntamente el suspiro último de la pubescente ninfa tribal.

Dinorah Cortés-Vélez

Applying for Citizenship

Here
folks
are my conditions:

English-only speakers
should pay higher taxes.

Welfare system
should be abolished
for big corporations.

America
should be dropped
from the name
of this country.

Absentee ballots
should be allowed
for undocumented workers
only.

The Statue of Liberty
should be moved
to LA airport
San Ysidro Boulevard
or someplace in Oklahoma.

The White House
should be moved
to Puerto Rico
the Congress to

Harlem
the United
Nations to
Wounded Knee.

Half of the billboards
in the country
should be given to poets.
The other half
to children.

People who say
this is the best country
in the world
should do volunteer work
for the homeless
or sing the national anthem
backwards.

Bibles
should be
in hotels
one day a month.

Every other day
authors and books
should include:
El Aleph
Salman Rushdie
Popol Vuh
Maria Luisa Puga
Karl Marx
Langston Hughes

Joy Harjo
Gloria Anzaldua
John Okada

Old Karl
has intimated
that he prefers Mondays.

Commercials on TV
should be limited
to one minute every hour

The Cuban national baseball team
should play in the major leagues.

Brooklyn should be the official
language of Brooklyn
Mi mami
the official language
of Miami.

All military forces
in foreign lands
should return by December 31, 1999.

They have the option
of staying in those countries
and blending in.

People who do not
use cars should be
given free monthly tickets
on an airline.

More petitions
when I become
a citizen of this
my
nation of others.

Rubén Medina

Paramour

The Avon lady couldn't ring to announce her arrival because our doorbell didn't work. It hadn't worked since we bought the house on East Third Street. She knocked gently.

Mami had been waiting for her in the front room and opened the door after the soft knock.

"My name is Kathy," she introduced herself. "*Pase*, come in," *Mami* welcomed the woman who was perfectly color coded from hair to shoes. She wore her blond hair in a page boy just an inch below her chin with blunt bangs in front. Her face was freshly painted, nothing overdone, pale blue eye shadow and hot pink lipstick that matched the soft sheen on her fingernails. Her plaid jumper of purples and wines also carried a subtle line of pink, the exact color as on her lips.

My Aunt Mina had bought lipstick and face powder from Kathy before. When Kathy asked Mina if she had any friends who might be interested in Avon beauty, *tía* Mina told her about *Mami*. Mina was to be at our house to break the ice. "If you bring other friends it'll be more fun," Kathy suggested. Mina said, "Of course, we have friends." Kathy knew how those things went. If you get them together, one will buy something and then the next one will until they're all counting their cash to pay.

When the appointed time arrived, Mina was already at our house with Berta from across the street and her friend Jovita. And then there was me, *para servirles*-- at your service. I was sixteen and was there to translate.

The five of us and the matching colors lady

barely fit in our tiny front room. With our big family, we also used the living room for sleeping. The couch was pushed all the way against the wall facing the front door. Across from it and to the right was the double bed with the bookcase headboard and a chest of drawers that was part of a set. We hadn't bought the vanity dresser with the mirror yet. With only a walking path between the foot of the bed and one end of the couch the two formed an L-shape, suitable for any visit.

"This will be just fine," Kathy said, looking around at the furnishings in the room. "Just fine," she said and tapped her hand on the arm of the couch. I stood in front of her, silently hoping that she not slap the couch again because, when she did, she had roused up a small cloud of dust. But Kathy hadn't noticed because she was busy convincing herself that "this is just fine." *Mami* and Jovita also sat side by side with Kathy on the couch.

"My name is Ka-thy." The Avon lady enunciated the two syllables of her name slowly, leaning her face towards *Mami* and Jovita to her left. "Ka-thy," she repeated towards Berta and Mina who sat on the side of the bed at a right angle to the couch.

"Ah, Kefy," Berta nodded and the rest repeated, "Kefy."

"Ka-th-th-y," she said, this time holding her tongue against her teeth for the "th" which clarified nothing and made her sound like she had a lisp.

"That's how they say it," I explained and Kathy decided to move on. On the TV tray that *Mami* had placed in front of the couch just for this purpose, Kathy spread her pretty bottles and pink compacts, explaining each as she went along.

Maybe because Kathy looked so pretty, I looked more closely at the clothes and the hair of *Mami* and her friends. Except for my Aunt Mina, they looked like they shopped for clothes by what was on the clearance rack. My Aunt Mina had her own style. She had a fresh Lilt perm in her hair and wore a beige straight skirt with a red and white striped blouse and red sandals that showed off chipped, painted toenails. *Mami* wore a blue and green plaid shirt-dress she'd made from remnant fabric from Ben Franklin. Berta was heavy from giving birth to eight children and had liver splotches all over her face from all those pregnancies. With each new baby, Berta's complexion got worse. She wore a corduroy housecoat, faded olive green, with snap buttons up the front. Jovita was the petite one of the four. She wore a pleated blue skirt with a white eyelet blouse that tucked in at the waist under a trim belt. As for me, that day I wore yard-sale hand-me-downs: a white blouse with a round Peter Pan collar that I pulled out over my navy-blue sweater. I could feel the label on the blouse collar scratch my neck, but at least I was wearing something store-bought.

Kathy picked up the eyelash curler because she wanted to demonstrate the mascara. "A volunteer?" she said, looking around.

Berta slapped her hand on her thigh and said, "Here I am. Make me over." She started to get up to move to the couch. But Kathy gestured with her hand, saying, "Stay right where you are."

Kathy moved towards Berta with the tool which *Mami* said, "Looks like part scissors and part garlic press but not a whole lot like either one."

"Actually," Berta said, "it reminds me of that instrument the doctor uses for women's examinations. *Ay*, they're so cold." I translated as much as I could for Kathy but when I had trouble coming up with the right English words, she motioned with her hand, palm up, telling me to stop.

"You don't need to translate everything," she said. "Just the basics is all I need. Otherwise, I could be here all day," she said with a sigh. I was happy to oblige since it's not easy to translate all the nuances and so much gets lost in translation.

"The trick is to catch your lashes between these two blades." Kathy pointed at the space in the tool in her right hand. "Then I'll squeeze to curl. That will make your eyes bigger, more open." As she explained, she held the fingers of her right hand pressed together then opened them up like a tulip to demonstrate the effect. "Then I'll brush on mascara for a finished look."

Berta rubbed her hands together, but then couldn't hold her eyes still. She blinked as soon as the speculum neared her eyes and jerked her face away. "It's a good thing I can't see it coming at me when I'm at the doctor's," Berta told the others. "With legs up, feet in stirrups with nothing but a bleached sheet between the doctor and a woman's honor," she said. *Mami* and Jovita threw back their heads and laughed. Mina started to laugh but stopped herself when she noticed Kathy standing there waiting. Because I had not translated what

Berta said, Kathy was left looking from the women to me with a blank look in her eyes, her jaw slightly dropped.

"What'd she say?" Kathy asked and squinted her eyes at me and at Berta.

"Control yourself," Mina scolded Berta, "you're not a girl." Berta regained her composure because, as she said, "I want curled lashes." Berta leaned back on the bed bracing herself by the arm, her legs splayed slightly. Straining to keep her eyes open, she looked like a frog turned on its back. As soon as Kathy's hand got close enough to make her cross-eyed, her eyes started twitching again. So Kathy decided to skip the curling and move on to the mascara. That presented the same problem. Berta had to hold her eyes open long enough for Kathy to place the wand right under her lashes. Once Berta understood that she would not be squeezed but caressed, she stopped blinking. In fact, she got the hang of it quite nicely, blinking down sensuously as Kathy stroked the wand up, coating each lash with the color of *Cielo de Media Noche*, Midnight Sky.

"See, isn't she lovely?" Kathy's hand squeezed Berta from the base of her head and swiveled her head one way, then the other to show off her eyes to the rest.

Mina said, "*Mejor pero no hermosa.*" The other three nodded in agreement that she looked better but not lovely.

Jovita took the tweezers and moved towards *Mami* who surprised me by letting her friend pull out a few stray hairs from her eyebrow. "*¡Ay!*"

Mami yelled and pushed the tweezers away. "Don't pull out too many," she said. "I don't want to look like that country-western singer." Next Jovita evened out *Mami's* eyebrows with a special pencil that was also the color of Midnight Sky. Between short strokes, Jovita licked the point of the pencil, then applied more Midnight Sky color. I was glad Kathy didn't see Jovita licking the eyebrow pencil because it didn't seem right to me.

When Jovita reached for one of the other colors still in the case, Kathy held the palm of her hand out again and yelled, "Stop!" She shook her head over and over as if Jovita had been about to commit a serious mistake. "Not those colors," she told Jovita, "they're designed for fair skin not . . .." She stammered . . . "Those colors are not for women with your *olive* skin." Kathy stressed the word *olive*, pleased to have come up with a neutral word to describe the women's dark skin. I translated, telling them that, according to Kathy, their complexion was the color of *piel de olivos*. Following Kathy's lead, I also stressed *olivo*.

But *Mami* and the rest saw right through it. I could see by their blank still faces, followed by the quirky shift of eye contact between me and Kathy, that the fire was about to roar.

"*Piel de olivos*. Olive skin? Olive skin?" Berta and Jovita repeated this question in unison, Berta with her hands on her ample hips.

"I don't know about you," Berta directed her words to Kathy so I translated them, "but where I come from, olives come in green or black." She paused to let me finish translating. "And our skin is neither," Berta finished.

"Maybe she knows of special olives. . ." Mina started but Berta wouldn't hear of it.

"¡*Nada, nada, nada*!" She shook her finger from side to side at Mina. "There is no such thing. Olives are green or they're black. Isn't it so, *señoras?*" She looked to the rest and they nodded in agreement.

"It's only out of ignorance, bad education," *Mami* said, "that someone would compare our faces to olives."

Then *Mami* said, technically to Kathy but she didn't look at her which told me that I was not to translate that part: "*Ay tú*, ex-cuse me. Just because we're not *güeras,* we can't try the other colors." *Mami* and Jovita returned to the *Cielo de Medianoche* eye-brow pencil which *Mami* irreverently called, "*Cielo de Madrugada*, pre-dawn sky, because time's-a-passing and it can only be midnight for an instant, right?"

To smooth things over, I paged through the brochure to suggest other colors. Colors for lips and cheeks with names that made your lips pout and your neck stretch out like a swan's: Magnificent Mauve, Precious Plum, and Mostly Mocha. I pouted my lips and sucked in my cheeks to imitate the models in the pictures. "Look what she's doing," Berta said flipping her head up in my direction. *Mami* laughed and also tried to mimic the pout of lips and sunken cheeks.

Berta and *Mami* looked in the mirror after they had brushed on rouge, which in the brochure was called blush, and lipstick, which was called

gloss. One look in the mirror and they howled.
"*Ay*, it's too much!" Kathy handed them a special
white cloth to blot the excess. "Pat, don't rub.
Rubbing wrinkles, rubbing wrinkles," Kathy said,
taking the cloth from Berta and poking little dabs at
Berta's cheeks and under her eyes, wiping off rouge
where she thought it was heavy. Then she did the
same for *Mami*.

"There, isn't that better?" Kathy handed
them each a mirror.

Holding it by its handle, *Mami* gazed at
herself, angling the mirror then turning her head to
one side, then the other. She liked what she saw.
"*Mira nomás*," she said, still looking. She caressed
the side of her face smoothly with her hand, starting
from the cheekbone where Kathy had left the color
strongest, she followed the contour with the color
blending towards her dimples and vanishing into
nothing at her chin. "Look at that," *Mami* said to
Berta, who was enthralled with her own image in
the mirror.

"*¡Qué cosa!*" Berta admired herself, turning
her head and tilting her chin up for a complete view
of the line of her neck. "*Hasta se ve más delgadita
la cara. No tan cachetona*," Berta said slapping a
fat cheek. Then she squeezed her lower cheeks with
one hand which made her mouth pucker into the
mirror. I translated for Kathy, figuring she would
want to know: "Berta thinks the rouge makes her
fat cheeks look thinner."

"We almost look as good as the models in
the pictures," *Mami* said, paging through the
brochure again.

"*Ya no te chifles*," Mina said to *Mami*. I told Kathy what Mina said—that by comparing herself to the models, *Mami* was going too far.

"Much better, much, much better," Kathy said looking at *Mami* and Berta. Then she crossed her arms, satisfied with her work, and nodded at the same time.

Still turning the pages, *Mami* nudged me with her elbow. "Ask her to show us the bath powders and perfumes," she said.

I translated the request and also told Kathy, "My father doesn't believe in women painting their faces with make-up." Kathy didn't say anything. She was busy putting away her compacts and tubes in her case and opening a soft bag with flowers on the cloth.

"Why not?" she finally said.

"He says decent women don't paint their faces, unless they're planning to join the circus to become clowns."

Kathy laughed at my father and said, "If it's overdone, maybe. But if it's done right, you'll look better. They don't look like clowns, do they?" she said, pointing first to *Mami* then at Berta. I had to agree with her. "Of course they don't," Kathy finished.

"No offense," I said to Kathy, "but that's what my *Papi* says."

Mami poked me with her elbow again. "Does she have Tabu? I can't find it in this booklet." *Mami* asked, and explained that Tabu is a brand of bath powder she used to buy when we lived in Muzquiz, Coahuila but she hadn't been able to find it since we moved this far North. I wondered what my mother wanted with such a brazen body powder.

"That's made by a different company. I only sell Avon." Kathy dismissed the question about Tabu as she brought out her own demonstrator bottles of fragrance and round boxes of pink and white talc. Kathy turned to the page where the pictures of perfumes started: Mesmerize, Pearls of Lace, Sweet Honesty, and Rare Gold. *Perlas de Encaje, Oro Raro. . ..* I started to translate but Jovita covered my mouth with her hand to interrupt. "We only care about the aromas, not the names," she said.

"This is a special one." Kathy handed the bottle to Jovita who smelled it and wrinkled her nose, not sure if she liked it.

"It's called *Par-a-mour,*" Kathy enunciated each syllable of the perfume with feeling and paused to see if the women would react. I translated the name of the perfume for *Mami* and her friends: "It's called, *Amante.*" *Mami* and the rest looked alarmed. Finally *Mami* broke the silence saying, "It's a perfume for adventure."

Jovita tipped her head until her nose hovered over the top of the bottle, then straightened up. She said nothing.

"Well. . .? What do you think?" Berta said.

"It smells a little like jasmine," Jovita finally said, but she didn't sound convinced. She passed the bottle on to *Mami* who took a deep breath.

"Very little of jasmine," *Mami* agreed.

"Actually," she said, "it smells more like a bed that hasn't been made in two weeks." That made us all laugh with Berta falling back on the bed where she was sitting. Mina pulled at Berta's arm and said, "Sit up."

"Let me see," Mina reached for the bottle from *Mami*. "How can an Avon perfume smell of dirty linen?" But after grazing the open bottle under her nose, she didn't argue with the other two.

Berta was the last to take a whiff and made it unanimous. "The aroma of jasmine and wrinkled sheets. Jasmine and wrinkled sheets," Berta said. She slapped both of her thighs. The force of her laughter made her large breasts tremble under her housecoat. Kathy took the bottle back.

Seeing no sign of approval for the scent, Kathy explained, "The name says for love. *Por amor.*" Kathy pronounced the words in Spanish as best she could.

Jovita raised her eyebrows. She was the first to get it. "Oh, *para el amor*?" Jovita repeated the statement in the form of a question. Kathy handed the bottle to Jovita.

"Yes-yes-yes," Kathy said, sounding like a stuck record tripping on the same word. She nodded her head vigorously which made her perfect page-boy style bounce, without a single strand of hair shaking out of place. "Feelings from the heart," Kathy cupped her hand over her heart and went on. "It's a scent that allures." She held the sound of the "u" like a pigeon cooing and lifted her eyes to the ceiling.

With a spark in her eye, Jovita spread her

legs and lifted her skirt. "Let me squirt a mist of this Paramour up the river of love," she said. She reached with the bottle under her skirt. "That's where the heart is, isn't it?" she said. She waited for the others to agree with her but they couldn't speak. They couldn't believe what she was doing in front of the *americana*. But Jovita didn't stop there. "Whenever there's talk of love, he always ends up here," Jovita flipped the blue cloth near the hem to show she meant under the folds of her skirt. "That's why I've concluded," she said, "that the heart is below the waist, not above." I hadn't translated any of this last part for Kathy even though no one told me not to. My silence left Kathy with a puzzled look in her eye. She turned from one woman to the other, her eyes blinking rapidly, as if hoping that by clearing her eyes she might extract meaning from the Spanish words she didn't understand. In a few seconds, Kathy grabbed the bottle of Paramour from Jovita's hand.

Berta and Mina looked around with hands at their mouths to conceal mischief and pleasure. *Mami* kept her lips tight until she couldn't contain herself. "The heart," she said before sharp bursts of laughter erupted from her mouth. "*El corazón,*" she repeated then tried to recite, "*Adiós corazón de arroz. . .*" Her laughter interrupted her but she picked up the verse again, "*Si te veo mañana me caso. . .*" She laughed again and couldn't finish it. I knew how the rest went: "*Adiós corazón de arroz.*" *Si te veo mañana me caso con vos.*" It was from an old story *Mami* had read to us years ago. The father in the story recited the verse to the mother, with affection, when he left for the day, or to his daughters if he dropped them off at a birthday party. *Goodbye my heart of rice. If I see you tomorrow, I will marry you*, I had literally translated the lines.

When I first heard that rhyme, I had pictured the heart as a patty that fit in the palm of my hand, a crumbly rice-cake. I liked the limerick so much that I made up an English version, one that rhymed: *Goodbye my rice-cake heart. If I see you tomorrow, we never shall part.*

Finally *Mami* stopped laughing. She turned to me and said that Jovita was only being playful. "Sometimes when people are that *honest*," she paused, searching for the rest of her words, "their talk sounds indecent."

Then *Mami* told me there were dishes in the kitchen that she wanted me to wash. From the kitchen, I could hear *Mami* chuckling, now that she had satisfied her obligation to mother me properly. Through the sound of water running in the sink, I heard *Mami's* low, muffled voice. "My daughter is a *señorita* of virtue," she explained to her friends. I rinsed a plate and placed it in the rack to drip dry. I shut off the water. *Mami* was still talking about me. She said she didn't want me exposed to "life's realities" yet and that I shouldn't hear about "the intimacies between a man and a woman."

From where I stood, putting the dishes in the cupboard, I could see that the women were all standing, saying their *goodbye's* to the Avon lady by the front door. *Tía* Mina had bought a tiny circle of rouge. Jovita held her sample of Paramour in a foil-sealed pouch and *Mami* bought a bottle of pink body lotion that cost a lot more than Jergens.

After the Avon woman left, I heard them in the living room talking and laughing, their giggles boisterous and out-of-control. One of them stomped her foot up and down on the floor, it got that rowdy. With the steel-wool pad, I scrubbed the inside of the black iron kettle where it had started to rust in places from sitting out too long with smears of mashed pinto beans on the inside. When I turned the kettle upside down on the rack, I heard Berta say, "Look at him, *muy güapo*, lounging on the bear rug with his little thing droopy and shy." She could barely finish her sentence because she exploded into a squeal of giggles again. Apparently the rest of them agreed with her by the sound of their laughter. Jovita returned to her earlier theme, the one that had sent me to the kitchen to clean dirty plates.

"What did I tell you? There's the *heart*." Jovita spoke with much satisfaction, as if she believed that her earlier point had been proved in the same visit.

With that, I couldn't resist. I took one step into the living room to see what could be *that* funny.

There was my mother sitting on the couch with the open pages of a *Playgirl* magazine draped on her lap. A naked man sprawled the width of two pages. She leaned her head over the picture and Berta and Mina, who had moved from the bed to the couch, were squeezed one on each side, staring at the naked man on her lap.

Jovita stood in front, bent over the picture.

She licked her thumb and index finger to turn the page.

"Not yet," *Mami* said spreading her hands over the pages.

"There's another one towards the back," Jovita said. "He's even better. I think he should be in the middle pages." Jovita turned page after page until she got to her favorite.

"Look at that," Berta said. "What have we here?"

"Uh-uh-huh! My-my-my," Jovita said.

"Uh-huh!" "Uh-huh!" The others moaned, as if they were eating sweet mangos. By reflex, I backed out before they knew that I had seen.

I was embarrassed. And disappointed with my mother. I could handle Jovita spraying perfume into her *calzones* under her skirt. She could make her panties smell good if she wanted. But the naked man on *Mami's* lap was something else. I wanted to walk out the kitchen door until they finished with their giggling. But I could not leave or *Mami* would want to know where I was going, and why, and I wouldn't be able to face her. I was trapped, standing over the sink, staring at the dirty dishwater where three bloated pinto beans, left over from lunch, floated near the top. Pulling the plug, I reached for the dishrag through the filmy water and wrung it, twisting every last dribble with quick tight turns. I endured the rest of their talk from the kitchen.

"*Esta revista. . . .*" It was Jovita, the worst rabble rouser of the four, whose voice I heard again. "This magazine is better than any perfume in Kefy's pretty floral bag. A few seconds of this and right away you get *ganas*." She snapped her fingers to indicate that immediate desire was yours if you just looked at the pictures of the pretty boy. I couldn't believe they were talking like that with only six feet and a thin wall between them and me. I took two steps towards the living room, thinking that if I walked through, they'd remember that I was there and that I was a *señorita* not a *señora*. From the door, I saw them in the same place again. Decency had made me timid, so I stepped back and resumed putting the pots and pans away. I made quite a racket, clanging the pans like cymbals as I stacked them in the lower shelf. I arranged and re-arranged the glass mixing bowls, nesting the smaller one inside the larger one over and over, trying to distract them with the noise.

Only when they heard the long horn of the Amalgamated Sugar Factory marking the end of the day shift at 4:00 p.m. did they decide to put the centerfold away. That day, I especially noticed the sadness of the horn, like a warning through fog. Outside, though, the weather was sunny and dry.

"My husband's coming home in ten minutes," *Mami* said with alarm. I heard Jovita rustle the pages of the magazine shut.

"Don't stuff it in your bag yet," *Mami* said. "Can I borrow it? I'll give it back to you next week."

My mother—the woman who hung the panties and brassieres out to dry on the line between the shirts and skirts so the neighbors didn't get a look at her undies—wanted to look at *Playgirl* for a solid week. Maybe, I hoped, Jovita would not let her keep the magazine because Jovita needed it for *ganas*. But my prayer went unanswered.

"Keep it as long as you want," Jovita said. "I've got the one from last month at home."

My mother's friend owned a subscription to *Playgirl*!

At the door, Jovita said to *Mami*: "If Nano sees the magazine, don't tell him where you got it."

"Don't worry," *Mami* assured her. "He won't see it. I'll keep it under the mattress."

In the kitchen, I cradled my forehead in my hands. My mother was going to keep other naked men under the same mattress where she slept with *Papi*.

I wanted the magazine out of our house. But I could do nothing about it. I wasn't supposed to know anything about the subject, let alone the particulars of that conversation. When they left and *Mami* started to walk toward the kitchen, I went in the bathroom. Just to stand there. In the mirror above the toilet, I noticed that my face looked like I had cried. So I washed my face with cold water and dried off with a towel, still stiff from drying out on the line. The scratch of the towel against my face felt so good that I rubbed long and hard. Studying my face in the mirror again, I brushed a flake of dry skin above my eyebrow with the towel. The words of that rhyme came back to me: *Adiós corazón de arroz* . . . From deep inside, a quiver rippled through my arms and legs. Then I stood still, hoping that the feel of the last hour would evaporate.

When I walked back in the kitchen, *Mami* was lifting the sack of flour from the bottom cupboard to make the *masa* for supper's *tortillas*.

"Can I help you with something?" I offered, not looking her in the face.

"You can peel five garlic teeth and dice this onion for me." She placed the garlic and onion on the counter next to me.

Without looking at her, I brought up the cutting board, took the knife, and began my attack on the onion, making quick, quick chops to block out my thoughts. Now and then, when the memory of the minutes before sneaked in, I lifted the knife as high as my head and brought it down with a whack.

"Careful you don't cut yourself," *Mami* said, looking in my direction.

I ignored her and went on with the dicing. Quick, quick, quick, quick, WHACK! Maybe tomorrow, I could look at my mother again. Chop, chop, chop, chop, WHACK!

Teresa Elguézabal

Frijoles and a Macho Sandwich with Papitas on the Side!

AYYY CHICANA!!!

Caught in between fathers, brothers, husbands, lovers and sons on one side and priest, bankers, bosses and "whoever else" you are dealing with today, tomorrow or next week.

When is it your turn to sit and be served at the table? Did anyone know that you were hungry?

When is it your turn to put up your feet to drink coffee and watch t.v.? Did they see the clean floor?

When is it your turn to take out a loan to buy a car? Oh, are you taking a bus to the doctor, are you sick?

When will you be "head of household" at the same time you bring in the money while your man stays at home? What, are you working?

When is it your night out at the bars, without questions asked? Do you have friends?

And, hey,
When do you get to wake-up the person next to you and say NOW?! Do you need something?

AYYY CHICANA!!

We like the Frijoles at the meal, they "gotta" be there, but who cares if anybody eats them! They make the meal whole but who takes notice of them unless they're sour!

They are a must, to hold everything together but

they never stand alone!

And,
the papitas on the side, well, they're a must, for
flavor!

Rosa Salinas-Hultman

Porque te fuiste

Pienso en ti:
cuando me acuerdo;
cuando cantan los pájaros;
cuando la gente calla.

Pienso en ti:
cuando se levanta la luna;
cuando se despierta el sol;
cuando me doy cuenta de que ya no estás.

Pienso en ti:
cuando al almorzar no comes junto a mí;
cuando el césped del jardín pide tu espalda
      almidonada;
cuando las aceras no sienten más tu peso.

Pienso en ti:
cuando mis ojos giran con el vaivén del agua;
cuando el viento me golpea la vista;
cuando las hojas caen.

Pienso en ti:
cuando los grillos cantan;
cuando los peces vuelan;
cuando el tiempo se detiene.

Pienso en ti:
cuando duermo y no en sueño;
cuando miro y no te veo;
cuando la noche enmudece

P ienso en ti:
cuando te toco y no te siento;
cuando te hablo y no me escuchas;
cuando te pido un favor como si a un fantasma.

Pienso en ti
porque no sé qué pasará.

Pienso en ti.

Alfonso Zepeda-Capistrán

Because You Left

I think of you:
when I remember;
when birds sing;
and people fall silent.

I think of you:
when the moon rises;
when the sun awakes
 and I realize you are no longer here.

I think of you:
when I eat my lunch alone;
when the summer lawn awaits your powder white
    back
and the sidewalks no longer feel your weight.

I think of you:
when my eyes follow the rise and fall of the waves;
when the wind blinds my sight
and the leaves fall.

I think of you:
when the crickets chirp;
when fish fly
and time stops.

I think of you:
when in a dreamless sleep;
I look for you and you are not there
and the night has no more words.

I think of you:
when I touch you and I can't feel you;
when I speak and you don't hear me

and I ask you for a favor as if to a ghost.

I think of you:
not knowing what will pass.

I think of you.

Alfonso Zepeda-Capistrán

Toward You

I pull toward you
as the tides toward the moon.

Constant, like the waves on the shore
But just as changing and new
in the treasures brought up
from the deep waters,
Waters I had watched from the same shore,
Never before feeling invited to dive
and now received so lovingly
in that ocean we claim for our own.

You, as beautiful and shining
as the moon
Caressing my waters and
bringing me to ecstasy
as the moon to the tides.

Debra A. Martinez-Hutchins

The Other Woman

One spring day, it always happens in spring
one spring day, out of the blue
the other woman
popped into my life.

I wasn't looking for a relationship
no one really is, but the first time
I held her, I thought I was going to
squeeze the life out of her, but I didn't.

She is a good listener,
keeps looking into my
eyes and laughs when
I am happy. One can't ask for more in a friendship.

Its hard to explain,
but she is calling me at
all hours of the night,
just what I need
a fatal distraction.

I used to believe
honesty is the best policy
But I am afraid to lose
both of them, for the love of one.

I think my wife knows
something is going on,
but I don't know what to do.
or worse how to undo

what's been done.

it is the nineties
and I am sure this
thing happens all the time
to somebody else
but not me, not now

but what should I expect
from a three-week-old baby girl
my daughter Lorena Pilar Barbosa-Mireles
the other woman
in my life.

Oscar Mireles

The Last Serenade

Tía Natalia looked out the window and mumbled: "If God had intended for us to have Santa Clauses, He would have given us snow." I was sitting at the dining room table. Some scattered pots hung on the wall from nails and a brand-new sink, which Tío Ancelmo and Tío Carlos had installed a few days before, shined when the sunlight came through the window. Even though I couldn't see any farther than the kitchen walls, I knew Tía Natalia must have seen Tío Ancelmo. Tía Natalia's comments about Santa Claus and snow had become part of Tío Ancelmo's annual visits. I even remember the first time I heard her say her now-famous comment. That Christmas, Tío Ancelmo brought me a big doll dressed in a white, long-sleeved blouse, a red plaid skirt and boots. I also remember his bemused expression when confronted with the fact that he was two gifts short. He took off his hat, scratched his head and exclaimed, "Two more!" Both Tía Lourdes and Tía Mercedes had their new babies in their arms.

"They don't know anything about Christmas yet," both tried to assure Tío Ancelmo.

"Besides," said Tía Natalia, "there's always Three Kings' Day."

"My plane leaves the second of January," answered Tío Ancelmo. I can't remember the rest of the argument but I do remember the feeling of uneasiness and Tía Natalia finally blurting out her comment about the snow and Santa Claus.

Two days later that Christmas, brothers and

sisters sat around the dining room table while we kids were made to sit on grandmother's sofa. She had died during the summer. There wasn't much talk except for deciding who was getting what, this I understood later, and the argument about the photograph.

"I think it is only fair that I get it."

"Fair? Maybe we should discuss who's getting it, Natalia," said Tío Ancelmo, looking around the table, hoping for some sympathy for his cause. I could see the picture from where I was sitting. In it grandmother smiled, still a young woman. As I heard the story later, the picture was taken between the two pregnancies that resulted in the births of my two youngest aunts.

"You weren't even here when she died," Tía Natalia blurted, while glaring at Tío Ancelmo from above her glasses.

"I took an airplane as soon as I could," Tío Ancelmo defended himself. I was five years old then. That day not even Tío Carlos joined forces with his oldest brother. The picture remained where it was for another seven years.

Tío Ancelmo lived most of his life in the States and he only visited us during Christmas time. Ever since I can remember, he would show up around mid-December, loaded with Christmas gifts, which of course made my cousins and me jump with joyful anticipation of the holidays. Tío Ancelmo even resembled the chubby, jolly figure of Santa Claus that we began to see on Tío Carlos' television. For this reason we baptized him Tío Santa Claus. Of course, we never dared to call him

Tío Santa Claus in front of the grown ups, especially Tía Natalia, who, being the older female of the family, exercised a certain degree of power over brothers, sisters and their offspring.

As I grew older I found myself looking forward to Tío Ancelmo's arrival and to hearing his voice demanding *arroz con gandules* and *pasteles*. My mother smiled as soon as she saw him. She would go into the kitchen, where she had been preparing for Tío Ancelmo's arrival since the previous week, the pots and pans coming and going, every single dish out of the cupboard and not a speck of dust left for the most Spartan spider to build a web. It was one of the very few times I remember seeing my mother smiling so openly. Most of the time a sad expression covered her face, I guess reflecting the emptiness my father's untimely death left in her. I think this was one of the reasons why I looked forward to Tío Ancelmo's visits. Seeing my mother smiling was a precious gift and I didn't care if it came from Santa Claus or the Three Kings.

After dinner, Tío Ancelmo always asked for the cuatro. My mother would go into the bedroom and bring out the instrument from where it had been resting since the previous Christmas. Tío Ancelmo slowly tuned the twelve strings of the cuatro. As he worked on tuning it, I sat next to him and looked at both him and the cuatro. I guess the odd couple that big, chubby Tío Ancelmo formed with the delicate, small guitar may have appeared kind of funny to someone who happened to glance at them. After tuning the instrument, Tío Ancelomo began to play, his fingers moving fast from one position to another, creating sounds I didn't think it was possible to get out of the cuatro. Then there wasn't anything funny about Tío Ancelmo and his cuatro, but some kind of magical spell, dispersing celestial music as the evening began to fall. Eventually my mother called us in but we always managed to play just one more tune.

There were many times during those years when my mother offered the instrument to Tío Ancelmo. This was usually after one of his playing sessions. The first time I heard my mother offering to let Tío Ancelmo take the cuatro with him, a loud, chilling no came out of my mouth. They looked at me and I could see the same shocking surprise that was traveling through my body on their faces. That evening, I was sent early to bed. Neither of us realized my fear that if Tío Ancelmo took the cuatro with him to that mysterious place called New York, he would be gone forever, just like my father. For me, having the cuatro in the house was the guarantee that Tío Ancelmo would be back the following Christmas.

When Tío Ancelmo wasn't playing the cuatro, he wandered off around the family farm. The family farm was actually a joining of several smaller plots of land that the brothers and sisters had slowly acquired through the years. It wasn't always like this. Many years before, during World War II, my grandmother had became a widow, with no money, no skills and six children to support. The oldest of those six children was Tío Ancelmo, followed by Tía Natalia. Tío Carlos was the third oldest, then my mother and my aunts Lourdes and Mercedes. Finding himself, at the young age of seventeen, as the man of the house, Tío Ancelmo decided to try his luck in the States. He sold his cuatro and away he went. Soon after arriving, he wrote back to the family. Tía Natalia still has the letter and a couple of times she has shown it to me. In it he informed his mother that he had gotten a job washing dishes and chopping potatoes and carrots. In his next letter he sent them some money. After that, he sent back whatever money he had left, while longing for his cuatro during the short, gray, cold days of winter in his new place of residence.

Tía Natalia went on lifting pots and pans around the stove and I discretely got up and looked out. I didn't want to start another argument with Tía Natalia. Not while Tío Ancelmo was visiting. Sure enough, Tío Ancelmo was sitting under the flamboyán tree, playing the cuatro. Tío Ancelmo always did this in the afternoons. He sat and played tunes I hadn't heard for a while. The moment I heard a note or two the tunes came back to me and stayed in my mind, whispering an invitation to sing along. The cuatro had belonged to my father, though I have no memory of having heard him playing the instrument. My father died in an accident when I was a child. A truck loaded with sugar cane on its way to the mill turned over, claiming his life. I didn't get to know him, though the rest of the family was doing a fairly good job at scolding me, reprimanding me, advising me and looking out that I didn't take a wrong turn in life. I think one of the reasons I liked being with Tío

Ancelmo was because he didn't scold, reprimand or advise me. He just let me sit down and listen to him play the cuatro while my mind constructed far-away worlds to the rhythm of his music.

That evening at the dinner table, I asked Tío Ancelmo to teach me how to play the cuatro. Tía Natalia looked at me from under her glasses.

"Proper young ladies don't play the cuatro," she said in a harsh voice.

I had turned twelve years old the previous month and felt I was very capable of making my own decisions as to whether or not to learn to play the cuatro. Tía Natalia had declared me an "argumentative child"; we had had some arguments about the clothes I wore. I was about to defend my position when Tío Ancelmo's voice surprised us all.

"For heaven's sake, Natalia, it is not like she is proposing to elope with the boy next door." It was the first time Tío Ancelmo spoke like that to Tía Natalia since the incident of grandmother's photograph.

"Well, what do you think, Miriam," Tía Natalia asked, hoping that my mother would join her and make a common front against Tío Ancelmo.

"Well . . . the cuatro just gathers dust when Ancelmo is away." Tío Ancelmo and I won the battle. That night we sat under the flamboyán tree and he taught me the first notes. The instrument, though, seemed to have aligned with Tía Natalia and the sounds I was getting out of it didn't resemble at all the ones Tío Ancelmo got when he stroked the strings. We didn't feel defeated, though, and Tío Ancelmo went on trying to teach me how to play a simplified version of "Preciosa." This was Tío Ancelmo's favorite song, he told me, because it proclaimed the grandeur of Puerto Rico. For the next week and a half he patiently guided my fingers over the cuatro's strings. By the time Tío Ancelmo left, my music was beginning to sound more harmonious and my fingers seemed to know just where to press the strings more often than not. I spent the whole year "playing with the instrument," as my mother and Tía Natalia referred to my practices under the flamboyán tree.

Tío Ancelmo, and his gifts, came back the following December. I was very exited about this visit. This time I had a gift for him. I had finally learned how to play "Preciosa" and I was going to play it for him. The evening of his return I did just that; not without the intrusion of a couple of wrong notes, but I could see Tío Ancelmo had approved the effort. He listened attentively, even to the wrong, intrusive notes that tried to steal my show. Then he left the house, after patting me on the head and telling me how beautiful it was. He was out of the house for a long time. The evening was beginning to fall and the December air had a crisp feeling to it. I went outside looking for him. I found him sitting under the flamboyán tree. As I approached the tree, I could hear the singing of the coquies. I stood behind the tree but somehow he knew I was there.

"Come out, Rosalba. I know you're there."
"Isn't it beautiful?" Tío Ancelmo looked at me.
"The coquies," I said. "It's as if they were

serenading the stars and the moon." I didn't realize it then, but Tío Ancelmo was looking older and more tired than the previous year.

"I like that. A serenade to the stars and the moon." He paused, thinking of the words. "The serenade I've been missing." This time it was I who didn't understand.

"There are no coquies in New York," he informed me.

"The nights must be very quiet, then?" I sat next to him, like when I listened to him play.

We looked up to the sky. The stars had an intense shining to them that evening.

"No. Just other kind of noises. But not of coquies."

"Then you missed the coquies?"

"Yes, very much so. Though it took your voice and your song to make me aware of that."

"Why do you live over there if there are no coquies?"

"I don't know. People are creatures of habit." He patted me on the head again and told me it was time to go inside.

"You could always come back and stay with mami and me," I said as we walked toward the house. My heart pounded at this possibility but Tío Ancelmo didn't answer.

Next morning after breakfast Tío Ancelmo left the house to go for a walk. My mother saw him leave the house.

"Tío Ancelmo seems sad this time," she said after Tío Ancelmo left the house as we washed the breakfast dishes.

"He misses the coqu;oies," I told her. My mother looked at me with a puzzled expression on her face. "He misses listening to the coquies. He told me last night."

Tío Ancelmo didn't come home for lunch. For dinner we all were together, wondering where he could be. I saw him first, carrying a cluster of bananas he had picked from one of the trees on the farm. There were some ripe ones and we tried to go after them but Tía Natalia stopped us, giving us a stern look. Tío Ancelmo put the bananas down and looked at us.

"Well, family, if that is all right with you, I think this time I'll stay. I don't want to miss the last serenade." He looked at me while everyone was looking at him. The family consensus after his announcement was that Tío Ancelmo was getting old. He needed a warmer climate and someone to look after him. I knew there was more to it. I saw it deep in his eyes when he announced his decision. Tía Natalia must have seen it, too, even if she didn't say anything aloud. For Three Kings that year, she gave grandmother's photograph to Tío Ancelmo. I watched them both as they made place for it in Tío Ancelmo's room. They fussed with it until it hung just the way they wanted it. Then they stepped back and looked at it. For the first time since my fifth birthday I saw them hug each other.

"I know you would have preferred to be here...," I heard Tía Natalia whisper.

"Yes, I would have preferred..."

Tío Ancelmo lived with us for another six years. He died the year I was to start my music studies at the conservatory. He left behind the memories of late afternoons filled with the notes of his music-memories that have nourished my life as a composer. In his testament he declared me his only heir of the few dollars he managed to accumulate, with the condition that I continue with my musical training. As I listened to his last will, I remembered him sitting under the flamboyán, playing the cuatro. I wondered how many of his compositions were scattered through the air, flying free, searching for a soul that could truly understand them. The "few dollars" he refered to, turned out not to be that few. The money Tío Ancelmo left almost covered my four years of training at the conservatory. He also left me a letter. In it he asked me not to wait until my last serenade to discover who I was. It was the first thing I remembered next fall when I packed my suitcases to move to the boarding house near the conservatory.

Nydia Rojas

Something About Friendship

i am
given the simple pleasure
of language
and the comfort of your eyes
upon mine
knowing i may come in
from the cold
and the mad dark
and my strange weather
and find your heart
my shelter

Anthony Morales

That Place

That place
where we reach in
to catch water
cold and clear
as it escapes
down rocks worn
into steps.

That place
free-breathing and green
a shelter, for our needs
and our knowing.

I touch my hand to your tongue
after I have reached into
where the water
starts, and life shifts.

I see other worlds
in that place.

Debra A. Martinez-Hutchins

Coffee and Cookies

The goal of their lovemaking was not so much
pleasure as the sleep that followed it.
<u>The Unbearable Lightness of Being</u>
Milan Kundera

Love
> Verbal thickness
> loosened
> with swollen tongue

> Merciless executioner of emotions
> Tourturer in the Dirty War of hearts
> Butcher of human feelings

> Blinded angel
> genetically lost
> between Wall street
> multilingual bordellos
> and sacristies

> Cerebral arrhythmia
> of suffering loners
> Emotional tic
> inherited from sadness
> Opportunistic deformity
> sower of pain
> Utilitarian passion to give oneself
> Impossible desire to feel the world's jugular
> with the Other's fingers

> Postorgasmic "I love you" without reply

Inescapable feeling that in a long game there
is always room for revenge

Hungry body that begs
calculating mind that gives

Sightless search for the mirror in another

Liking red
Accepting green

Pedestrian happiness of waking up to coffee
and cookies
Flag hoisting in routine's country
Wish to be the sea which the Other's boat
endlessly explores

To become.

Rino Avellaneda

Café y Galletas

The goal of their lovemaking was not so much
pleasure as the sleep that followed it.
The Unbearable Lightness of Being
Milan Kundera

Amor

Espesura verbal
destrabada
con inflamada lengua

Inmisericorde verdugo emocional
Torturador en la Guerra Sucia de los
corazones
Destazador de humanidades

Cegatón ángel
por herencia perdido
entre Wall Street
multilíngües burdeles
y sacristías

Arritmia cerebral
de padecientes solitarios
Tic emocional
heredado de la tristeza
Tara oportunística
sembradora de dolor
Utilitaria pasión por entregarse
Imposible deseo de sentir la yugular del
mundo con los dedos de Otro

Postorgásmico "te amo" sin respuesta
Ineludible sentir que en juego largo hay
desquite

Hambriento cuerpo que ruega
calculadora mente que da

Invidente buscar el espejo en otro

Gustar del rojo
aceptar el verde

Pedestre felicidad de despertar con café y
galletas
Izada de bandera en la patria de la rutina
Deseo de ser mar que el zozobrante bongo
del otro explore a más no poder

Llegar a ser.

Rino Avellaneda

Unselfish

To be myself,
There is a dance in my mind.
Not one emotion is away from the dancing floor.
All their movements demonstrate harmony.
There is no direction nor path.
It is my free spirit...
It is I
Who cries
I love you on my own free-will.

Rafael Gómez

In a Dream

Love with me
Fall into our bed
Dive into the ocean
and know one breath.

In a dream,
you walked toward me.
And your arms,
outstretched,
pulled me deep
inside your mouth, eyes.
My sleeping body
knew your touch
we lay in love
satisfied
until I woke.

Debra A. Martinez-Hutchins

Untitled

i want to tell you about this dream i dreamt
something quiet something about pleasure
something like you but no let me tell you
something else it's a clear night tonight and
there are languages i am dreaming on words to give
you to live inside you to fill you make you round
and living like the autumn moon did i tell you that
day i couldn't see you was awful and the night the
night made a dull ache in my chest and the morning
the morning you telephoned filled me but there was
something else some other meaning to this
phrases images moments i am trying to gather for
you something remarkable something about a dream
i dreamt this night this wide sky these open eyes
these thoughts coming to me leaving for you
sometimes being a poet can be a hurting beauty do
you know there was this dream this conversation we
had something about loss of human contact what it
means to breathe in skin to receive a tiny kiss a
holding hand and i remember saying don't lose this
don't lose me and waking up to this white moon this
clear night i wanted to tell you do you know what it
means for me to know you do you know how
you fill me but there was something else some
meaning some uncommon language between us
unexpected and affectionate our lives passing
through us our small ghosts meeting and there was
something more do you know this is what it means
to know you this is the effect on my body this is
how i care for you this night this moon this dream
saying don't lose this don't lose me tell me do you

believe in spirit desires do you know love do you
know romance do you have enough and do you
need more tell me do you know a clear night a
white moon all things are possible there was this
dream i met a little ghost a conversation in the
kitchen do you know how i love you let me tell you

Anthony Morales

To the One I Love

My heart is spitting these words at you.
My love is out of control.
My heart hurts my chest
When I think of you.
Is your heart true?
Am I a puppet in some cruel game
Or do you love me with a strong heart and an open
    soul?
I can't control this.
My heart burns.
I loved you always
I can't stop!
Help!
Save me!
Please!
Now my tears are out.
They want to kill me!
End this game!
I love you.

Michael Guerrero

Sonido

No hay salida para la palabra.
Quien la escucha hace juicio.
Ella sabe que no solo es sonido.
A veces le responden con el olvido.
Cuando se trata de amor puede
    Llevarnos al suicidio.

Ella tiene fuerza.
No te hagas nudos en la cabeza.
Escucha su sonido.

Rafael Gómez

Bandages

I.

My little soft hands are clinched so tightly

paper-thin nails drive into my palms.

If I squeeze them REAL hard so hard that I can't
    breathe

keep them closed so no air no light no lint can fit in
I can pretend without even knowing I'm pretending.

II.

There are secretos you keep from your friends,
cuz they would tell.

Secretos you keep from the world,
cuz they would call you names.

secretos you keep from yourself
cuz they could kill you.

III.

memories of you were wrapped up
in layers of bandages
which held my stitched up life together,

but the blood of our sins
seeped through
underneath it all

you were there
you were waiting
the cup of your hand guides my head

IV.

it was you my Popo
who turned into Cortez
invading.

V.

All these years
You have been crushed back
in half dreams,
half nightmares,
full lies

like a ghost trapped inside a house
you rattled within me
waiting for me to rediscover.

VI.

You didn't make this baby a woman
you didn't teach me what I needed to know

you said it was love
the kind of love you don't tell anyone about
cuz they wouldn't understand.

If this is love
yo no quiero.
but the irony is
i have spent my lifetime seeking it
destroying it
and men who were offering it.

VI

scrubbing and scrubbing
behind my knees,
underneath my eyelids,
every crevice of my cells,
but like an outdated tatoo
you permeate

I can't get away
I can't get away

poppi
look what you've made of me.

Tess Arenas

Brown and Blue

Most young children want to be firemen
or astronauts when they grow up
but that gets old pretty fast

it's very different when they say they want to be a
policeman,
it's more than an occupation,
they want to be "blue"
it's more than a career,
it's a lifestyle,
where one can be an Old West gunslinger
and carry portable metal death between your fingers
where one can be a bully, always in charge,
and can let the uniform speak for itself
it's living on the edge,
with red and blue light flashing for effect

yet the part of being "blue" that no one sees
is the boredom, the intense routine
of book-length police reports,
repeated delayed court hearings
chasing parking fines and tickets into file cabinets,
waiting for justice to come
into the smoke-filled hallways
watching criminals that get away
because the laws are made to serve not protect
this is the part that gives you the blues

Tony Morales knew what he wanted
to be when he was thirteen
which I think is dangerous

for anyone to admit
what they want to be at thirteen
'cause now it can change
'cause how can anyone know what they want to be
until they've messed up their life
a bit

The rites of passage to be Latino
nowadays aren't so clear
one can get away with
not speaking Spanish very well
or knowing all the traditional holidays and fiestas
or not liking hot sauce
or knowing all the chic Mexican restaurants

the rites of passage to
be a policeman are painfully clear
at least twenty-one years old,
good moral character
spend six months at the police academy
know how to properly salute
and shoot 250 on the marksmanship test

The problem for Tony was
it was too clean, too clear
just like the spit shine on his black shoes
there was no mistake
in knowing that he was going to fail his final test
no retest or make-up exam would ever change that
and at the age of twenty-one,
barely old enough to own a car payment
he would fail
the marksmanship test for the third time

this test of eye-hand coordination
that could be improved
by plugging a few quarters
into a video machine
and everyone in the room
would know he failed,
just by the silence

and Tony didn't take the time
to look around
for any signs of compassion

He pointed his gun
toward the tip
of his temple
the closest spot to the heart
of his mind
and broke the laughter
echoing in the basement shooting range
by splashing pieces
of his brain
and scalp
on the trembling walls
on his blue
police
cadet
uniform
that finally slumped
to the ground
with relief

Oscar Mireles

Lupita: La Hija de Juan

It is fateful and ironic how the lie we need in order to live dooms us to a life that is never really ours. Ernest Becker, **Denial of Death,** *1973*

I

There isn't a time when I don't feel somehow undone, incomplete, slightly confused, or just a little bit tinged. What appears to be just right for some always turns out to be just off for me. There are phases that take me on meaningless tracks, phases that take me off track and phases that are trackless. They are all slightly crooked. That's how I'd describe me, slightly crooked. Like a corner on a hanger that isn't right and needs to be bent back into its original curves.

I don't have any curves. Never really did. I like that. My angular shape keeps me light on my feet and quick. In gym class when the girls are looking for an easy target, they yell, "get Ramirez, get the little brown one." Grinning, I cut a line for the side of the court to escape the whoosh of the basketball as it brushes past my ear. I am sure a boy likes me for who I am (although I am on an endless search for true love) because I don't have any chichis. No tits, no ass; just me. In a test of love, I'm sitting on my teen angel's lap, inevitably he'll complain that my butt bones are stabbing him. If he asks me to shift a bit, I oblige and give him brazos almost choking him. Smiling to myself, I gloat, "he really likes me." If he asks me to get up, I know we are history.

As a young woman, being thin is my defensa against potential abductors, rapists, con men, mad men, just plain men. I dress in baggy jeans and working-class blue jean shirts, wear my hair like Los Beatles, and walk with a gait that doesn't give gender a chance to reveal itself. I am safe. I am an IT.

I have grown uncomfortably accustomed to the drama of my emotions; the laughter that wakes up the babies, and the sobbing that embarrasses those within hearing range. You don't want to be near me in the movie house when Doris Day tells Rock Hudson that she doesn't love him anymore. It takes me days to recover. To complicate matters, I'm a bit jumpy. I am the kind that can't stand a sneak-up. Unless you're prepared to scrape me off the ceiling, it's better to announce yourself before coming into a room.

That is just the way it is. I am the nervous one, the smart one, the oldest one, the one who checks the darkened doorway before she goes to sleep each night. The one that could "make something of herself if she just calm down. Cálmate, mija, cálmate."

II

Lupita is the first and frankly, my best work; the one that could probably land a decent husband, if any of us could. But she is mouthy. She probably got that from me. She tells the police they are pigs, tells the teachers to leave her alone, breaks up fights when boys with knives were trying for her brother Martin. Her and her brother. They are like one worm that had been cut in half. She resembles me and Martin resembles Juan. They were so cute together and fight like dogs for one another.

Juan loves to be around Lupita when he is in the house. He dresses her up in a fancy for-holidays-only dress and shows her off to his brothers and friends. Like she was a little puppy or something. She is the center of attention, La Reina he calls her. Then he'd go out with his buddies and forget to come home for two days. He doesn't like to come home during normal hours. At three in the morning he will walk in loudly demanding breakfast. So, there I am crying while making huevos con chorizo at 3:15 AM. And where is he when WE need him? Like the time Lupita fell down the stairs with her tricycle and cut her mouth so bad that the ambulance driver started crying.

I am so ashamed because I just can't control him. I can smell perfume and alcohol and get mystery phone calls from women. But no matter how hard I plead or how much I cry, he gives me a kiss on the forehead and tells me I am "getting hysterical and need to rest." When I leave him he promises to make it all better. I believe him. Six times I believed him. It is like I am hypnotized. I can't break free and I can't stand myself for it. During his bad times I can't even go out of the house because of the all the chisme. I can't stand their whispers. I want to shout, "Yes, he is malo, tan malo, pero watch out bitch, cuz he's hanging out with your old man."

What are you going to do? Anyway, with all Lupita has going for her, she was and still is so moody. Not crazy, just terminally emotional. She cries when she sees old men, she cries when she hears a sad song. Juan used to say that Mexicanos are the only people that cry to get happy, but it is more than that. When she gets depressed she has this routine she goes through. "What did I do to deserve this? Why do bad things always happen to me?". It is so damned frustrating. I just want to shake her and scream "snap out of it, stop feeling sorry for yourself and get on with your life."

I used to think that Juan left me. But Lupita lives her life as if he was leaving HER.

She should be grateful he didn't stick around to do more damage. It's better that she still remembers him as that handsome dark rigid shape she adores and who adores her-until he gets tired of being a husband and a father.

III

Being brown is very important to me. I am very grateful that I have my father's thick black hair. People comment, "her head glows blue in the light." But because my mother is a dark-haired anglo, my skin color is the part of me that raised questions. I am not morena. I am not ghostly como una gringa. I am medium tan half of the year and butternut in summer.

I am happiest in summer. There is something so serene about the damp light breeze that ripples through my window as I cuddle my bear in my sleep. I have this reoccurring dream each summer, about three times a week, that I can fly. Fly like a brown hummingbird. I am walking in front of my house with my magic bath towel cape that came free in a box of Tide detergent. Without any fanfare, I gently touch off the sidewalk, like a swimmer making a soft turn. My body lifts up weightlessly over the yards of the neighbors and baby birds squeak in delight and wave to me. I land where friends are making some heavy-duty mud balls. With eyes large as sinkholes, they ask me "How'd you do that?" To which I answer cavalierly, "Oh, didn't I mention it before? I fly." The power, the control, the total sense of freedom.

Laughing as they try to figure out my magic, I push off again and fly to the Grant Street School playground. There I fly above the hopscotch and four-square patterns humming softly and sweetly like my bird friends for hours.

In that dream I experience a calm that is constantly missing during my waking life.

If I have my wish, I will wake up one morning and my eyes will have gone from deep brown to rich black and my skin from peanut butter to milk chocolate. Then there would be no question who I am. What I am. Having been raised in the most segregated city in the country, most anglos are preoccupied about your origins, your right to live where you live, your right to take the bus to the other side of town. Wish I had 100 drachmas for every time an adult asks me, "Are you Greek?"

I call it the Anthony Quinn Syndrome. He played a Greek once, kinda looks Greek, but he is really Mexican. But nobody really wants to accept that so they stick with the Greek theory.

So I'd answer "No, Mexican."

"Oh. Do you speak Spanish?"

"No."

"Why not?"

"My father left when I was young and my mother is anglo, speaks a little, mostly swear words…That's why."

"Oooh. Sorry."

"No problem."

In less than 4 minutes I have divulged that my mom and dad broke the color line, my father didn't stay very long, and I'm the afterbirth of their adventure. I walk away with my cheeks burning and my heart throbbing.

Or I get a permutation of that conversation from my Mexican friend's family.

"Ramirez. Ramirez? Any relation to Juan Ramirez?"

"Yes, he's my father."

"Oooh. Which wife is your mother?"

"His second." (I later find out we are his third

family).

"I see. Your father is quite well known, you know. You look alot like him."

"Really, I think I look like my mom."

"Actually, you talk rapido just like him y tu eres suave como el tambien."

My smile would rim my eyes as I think silently, "Thank you. Thank you. Thank you."

Because half the world has difficulty figuring out who I am and who I belong to, I want to be dark, darker, darkest. Let me be so rich and deep that I seem to hover over the ground in radiance. Let the Español that sprinkles my thoughts multiply into a 1000 loaves to feed this constant craving. Then I'd believe in God. Well, maybe.

IV

Josefina calls me out of the blue and with a very strange edge to her already halting speech, "So, aahh, how you doing?" she asks.

"Fine."

"What's new."

"Nothing."

"So what are you doing?"

"Sitting around."

She begins to ask me another going nowhere question when I halted her with "what the hell is going on?"

"Well, Lucia Chacon called to tell me she saw a death notice in the newspaper."

"Who died?" I ask.

"I think it was your poppi," said Josefina.

"Are you sure? What did the obit say?"

"That Juan Ramirez, age 65, died of a heart attack and that he was a labor organizer in Racine."

"Wrong Juan. I think my poppi is 72 and was a community organizer in Milwaukee." I can breath again.

"GOD, I'm sorry. I hope I didn't upset you. Mujer, you just have too many fathers to keep straight." she said with a chuckle.

Hanged up the phone and laugh. But it isn't funny. Two fathers isn't too many. But what if Juan had died. I've had chances to meet him and inexplicibly I choose not to. I want to remember him my way; as the one that gives me the warm glow when he talked. The one that wraps me in his arm with the sleeve rolled up so I can snuggle in closer.

V

It started with a kind of nightmare. My fiancé, Michael, was drinking with a friend in the living room and I am in bed trying to get some sleep. I actually am asleep but I can still hear their laughter in the other room.

Suddenly, I am terrified. I need to vomit.
I think desperately, I have to get out of here.

I don't know why but I have to.

It isn't Michael. It is something or someone else. Some overpowering force that is so wicked, so horrifying that it throws me into violent waves of alternating sweat and nausea. If I can only wake up I could see that this is a dream - a very bad dream. There is nothing to be afraid of but nonetheless I am. I am like a child who can't protect herself when she wakes to find her house screaming on fire. I want to grab my bear and crawl into the closet to escape the wrath of the flames.

A bulky scream is stuck in the back of my throat. I gag. I squeeze my eyes closed to become invisible. Rolling into a fetal ball I push my face up against the wall. If he (WHO?????) comes in all he'll be able to touch is my back. I can feel his breath. Oh my God, push off! Push off! Where is my magic towel??

I am terrified in a waking state for 2 days and afraid to go to bed for many more.

VI

Then it is as if this dream/nightmare/Salvador Dali reenactment went on hiatus. After the birth of our beautiful daughter, Carmen, my world is complete. By the time she is two it starts in again.

Nightmares move on to memories. Memories start to reconvene arbitrarily over the next few months. They have the uncanny ability to ignore my surroundings and will just appear. A groping hand while eating dinner. A shoulder digging into mine while washing the dishes. The sound of a belt buckle. The crush of body weight. The stench of liquor. The bittersweet sperm and my tiny voice whimpering,"no poppi, no."

Within a period of 90 days my carefully constructed casa de las tarjetas life of 39 years shatters with razor cuts of truth.

My fear of unsolicited touch, darkened doorways, and drunken men now made sense.

My corners are straightened. But getting straight didn't feel good. It is hard to have life fall into line. I am alone. More alone than any daughter could ever be. It isn't just my sensitive nature that made me feel the pain so acutely. It is the 10,000 leagues under the sea mourning that comes with the death of a lie. My lie. Your lie. Our lie Juan:

I, Lupita Ramirez, remember now. You were in the doorway and you claimed me like some prize. Took my adoration and twisted it, like a corkscrew and pulled it out leaving me bewildered and devastated. Too confused and too young to sort it out.

I have spent the last year giving birth to my own life. A life that will not be manipulated by the after shocks of your definition of love. My child and my husband have suffered as they watched me fall into tiny pieces, dance with suicide and shudder in disgust. There have been months of nightmares, night sweats, night calls to help lines. To think that one single human being can penetrate the lives of so many innocent others from one generation and one relationship to another. You have been such a powerful force and such a devastating one tambien. I shrank away from the people that love me as I tried to sort this out.

When I finally told Josefina, she cried and said it was her uncle that initiated her. I told Socorro and she told me it was her grandfather who opened her. All this time we have been walking wounded and each of us went through the hell of healing by ourselves. I was the first to call them in on the pain. They were both the rocks that I needed them to be. They told me of their shame, their hatred, their anger. They kept telling me "when you get past the anger, you can say you've made it through the worst."

I waited for the anger for six months. I gave up on it actually. Then Michael said I was getting weird again.

She stood up on her hind legs and kicked out windows, doors, and walls, her mane flapping in the wind, nostrils emitting hot steam in the night as she catapulted out of the house. Mother Earth cried as she watched her daughter dig her maniacal cantor into the ground.

Then I dreamt that Michael and I killed you. It wasn't gruesome or perverse. We quietly and calmly decided that it was the best thing to do. It was over in a blink. No noise. No violence. Just done.

I am sleeping again.

I don't know where I'll end up on all of this.

Nor do I know which path will take me home.

Barbara Whitefeather asked me to go to a sweatlodge with her. Said I have been quiet and it might be time to give my thoughts back to the soil. Let mother absorb them.

I am starting to write again. I haven't been able to pick up a pen in years. It is interesting that the pain that closes me off from myself is the same pain that opens me up to my other self.

Please don't expect me to thank you for it.

Sin Cariño,

Guadalupe Inez Ramirez
(AKA La Hija De Juan)

I will never send the letter. But it helps me none the less.

I guess I can say that I am over of the worst of it. I realize the turning point comes with a revelation that instead of mourning the fact that you deserted me I should count myself among the lucky. Some girls have fathers like you into their teens. If I ever felt like praying it is now.

Thank you for taking him away.

VII

The obtiuary said Juan Ramirez, age 78, died on March 25, 1993 in Califas. Survived by children. I almost laughed.

You have so many they couldn't all be listed.

I've put your death on hold for a while. I don't know what I feel if anything.

My chances for confrontation are gone, my opportunity for possible answers has slipped away. But then again, would I ever have been given answers that gave me what I needed? Those elusive speckles of wisdom are floating out in the cosmos somewhere and my towel doesn't fly me that high.

Tess Arenas

Christopher

(In memory of my son)

You were the star that announced
the birth of our future.
You were the eagle that soared
through our horizons.
You were thunder and lightning,
morning dew and soft breezes.

You were the historian of
our past, present and future.
You were a cholo, a leader
and a warrior…
You were a macho, un hombre…
un caballero.

You are now our feelings
and our warm remembrance.
You are now the dweller
in the depths of our spirits.

So, it is time, my son
to rest from all your travels
and be cradled in our love
and our memories.

Gladis Benavides

Chuco Pachuco Carnal

for José Moreno

In the "colegio" where the establishment
sends our best Chicanos is where we met.
What was there for me to teach
you - against all odds you educated yourself
and stood taller than all of the guards
who kept watch so your soul would not escape.

Today, your sister wrote me:

... lo siento mucho a informale
que José pasó a la otra vida 16 meses atrás
pero antes se reconcilió con Dios.

Did God offer a better deal?
It was what you always wanted
to be
to be free
to be on the other side.
Curioso, the manila folder with your name,
containing tus cartas y poesías
inside the file cabinet
kept rising above the others like magic
or tratabas de decirme algo.
Me pongo loco trying to figure out
what it is you are telling me.

I remember how con tu sonrisa
you gently corrected me, the
teacher - pointed out "Hispanics are not in
        prison!

Raza, they lock up Raza," you said.
We laughed: I learned a lesson.

Rereading your cartas, anger overwhelms me
knowing the establishment is still crazy
locking up our Raza.
I want to tear down all the walls
melt down all the bars and chains
that for too many years incarcerates, locks away
... genuine souls like yourself

Your soul escapes ... taking a deep breath
my chest feels heavy around my soul.

Trinidad Sánchez, Jr.

Lone Figure

Lone figure looks out through second-story
    window, cracked glass, frost covered,
tears form ice rivulets along her face,
streetlight shines pale orange glow on new fallen
    snow, no tracks and she looks,
waits for his shadow, in this tiny circle of vision,
but all she sees is bars... in front of her, in front of
    him

lone figure looks out through tiny panes, denial
    planted firmly,
lodged midway between throat and belly, has no
    sound belonging to it,
in her hand she holds tightly a yellowed envelope,
    edges worn by salty palms,
ink blurred catching the runoff... he was her
    prince...
for a short time the story was about her...
and then they stopped coming...words...his were
    her life source...
she chewed them like a cow its cud... extracting the
    bittersweet juice of love...
savoring every sound and unspoken intention...then
    one day it thickened,
turned sour in her mouth and she could not swallow
and she could not let it go
what happens to a woman when she is rubbed raw
    against the steel bars of man's inhumanity,
they told me if i lay down and play dead they will
    not attack... again.
so i listen, against my breath... silence... broken by

sound …

church bells ring but they do not call him home… to
    me… to our bed…

i long… to smell him… to see his hands, his
    fingers…

his memory is fading against my need to survive…

life holds so strong to my ravaged body, molding
    between my ribs, sinking into my pelvis..

encasing me in its grasp and i cannot escape those
    bone fingers

and i am

alone

lone figure looks out through second-story window,
    her image filling the space of panes

and there is a shadow of a man who stands behind
    her, to the left,

his hand rests on her shoulder and tears flow
    endlessly,

carving their history against the granite face of
    reality…bone grinding against…

and the mark left…warriors graffiti, intersecting,
    intertwined, bound… by the blood of…

surviving in the shadows

Debra Barrera Pontillo

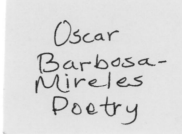

Mexican Roulette

Joaquin is dead,

He was listed on the morning radio
19 year old man who lived on the 900 block of
south 10th Street
shot in the head
with his own revolver
a victim of Russian Roulette

but there was no mention
of the fact that he had finished
his high school education in May of
last year, only one semester
after he was supposed to
when most of his teachers felt
his life would be finished
before the age
of seventeen

Or that he had worked at the community center two
years ago on a mural project in the front of our
building and was starting to see the connection
between the tattoos on his arm and the art hanging
on our walls.

Joaquin, could have been a bodybuilder
he had a solid rock body and a sense of humor,
Less than a month ago he volunteered to help
set up our annual street festival, all I had
to do was buy him a couple
of lunches and he was there
for three days with no complaints

Joaquin is dead
and I know who was with him
at the time of miscalculated fear
it was Cruz, not yet sixteen but not willing to stay
away from the violence
that surrounds him everyday
I know Cruz is scared, mad, angry
and wishes he could've done something
but it's too late

too late to take the gun away,
even though he took out the bullets

too late to tell Joaquin that manhood
is determined by what's inside your
heart and brain and you can't reach that
with a gun or a bullet

too late to change that second shot,
which went so fast it was unreal
too late for Cruz, who when he saw
the dead body he couldn't open up
the door and had to suffocate for three minutes
with the live stench of death

too late to fire the third shot
Joaquin deserved another chance
but maybe that is
the only thing
he can pass on now

Oscar Mireles

Olvidándote

Nadie sabe cuándo
comienza la vida
ni tampoco cuándo
llegue la muerte
solo se que un día
el olvido llegó
y se llevó tu sonrisa
de mi corazón
mi amor por tí
y se robó tu fotografía
de mi memoria
ahora estoy tratando
de recordar tu nombre
y cuando fue que te conocí.

Daisy Cubias

Forgetting You

Nobody knows
when life begins
or when death
will come
I only know
that one day
oblivion
took away
my love for you
erased your smile
from my heart
and stole your picture
from my memory
now I'm trying
to remember your name
and when it was
that I met you.

Daisy Cubias

Ode To Sharing

We shared
our first choking Marlboro,
Salsa and Samba Latin parties,
Dizzy nights diving into bottomless wine bottles,
Afternoon-long two-on-two basketball games.

We shared
Tall tales of the first sex,
Rib-breaking gang fights,
Greasy, cold late-night dinners of beans and rice,
Pierre Cardin sweaters to impress the girls.

We shared
Led Zeppelin and Santana records,
The loneliness of your fatherless home,
Fuzzy Santa Marta golden pot (the world's best),
The pain of your years of bottles of Diazepam.

Why didn't you ever talk of
Your tragic plans to climb the rope...
Jump
And
Break

The frailness
of your
neck?

Rino Avellaneda

Oda Al Compartir

Para saber cómo es la soledad
tendrás que ver que ya a tu lado no está
que nunca más con él podrás hablar
de lo que es el bien, de lo que es el mal

Leonardo Favio

Compartimos
nuestro sofocante primer Marlboro
rumbas latinas de salsa, vallenato y samba
mareantes noches zambulléndonos en inagotables
botellas de vino
tardes enteras de basquetbol en dueto

Compartimos
hermoseados cuentos acerca de nuestra primera
mujer el rompehuesos de juveniles barras en pelea
la fría grasa de arroz con fríjoles en cenas de
medianoche suéteres de Pierre Cardin para
impresionar a las muchachas

Compartimos
Música de Led Zeppelin y Santana
la soledad de tu hogar sin padre
rubia marijuana de la Sierra Nevada (la mejor del
mundo)
el dolor de tus años de Diazepam

¿Por qué nunca hablaste
de tus trágicos planes para
subir la soga. . .
saltar y

romper

                    la fragilidad
                    de
                    tu nuca?

Rino Avellaneda

The Vietnam Wall

With simple eloquence and beauty I saw his
name engraved on the wall we're off to
Vietnam to do our patriotic duty or did we? It's
hard to say I can't recall

left are the shattered bodies, hopes and dreams of
having to defend this Land for Uncle Sam by
fighting the Viet Cong and Communist regimes
pieces left behind in the countryside of Nam

youthful memories of growing up together near
Zacate Creek in the barrios of Laredo where war
was faraway from everything now it all seems
distant filled with words I can no longer speak in a
time before all innocence corrupted within our very
being

how can one help the hurt that rends inside one's
heart? for even after thirty years since I have lost
my boyhood friend the guilt of coming back - while
he did not - has torn me all apart why do I feel I live
on borrowed time? Someday I hope to comprehend

I waited for the words to come, but only felt the
piercing pain then as I glanced I saw my image
reflected in the marble roll then words came out,
why Lord, did Juan González die in vain? was it my
friend I grieved? or, was it, the loss deep down in
my very soul?

Juan Alvarez Cuauhtémoc

Untitled

It was when she was on a table, her legs spread wide open and a Vacuum-like tube sucking out what should have been her daughter that she had only one statement running through her mind.

Her arms were pinned down and her eyes were glued to the blue-eyed nurse who continued to try to distract her by making ignorant inbred-hick statements like "The weather's always so strange in Milwaukee this time of the year don'tcha think, sweetie?" Meanwhile, in front of her, a fat balding man with retro '60's glasses looked down at her privates holding some gadgets, whistling "working in a coal mine."

Out in the waiting room, her manipulative boyfriend sat and tried to keep his thought (and eyes, to ignore the gorgeous blonde receptionist) on a copy of rolling stone magazine. his father sat next to him, straightening the crease in his slacks, (eyeing the blonde receptionist), checking his watch, trying to show support, but really just waiting for all of this shit to be over and done with.

Meanwhile, back in the operating room, the tube is removed. the horrible sound of suction and the ripping of flesh is gone. the fat guy stands up and says "it's over. you're done." the blue-eyed, inbred-hick releases her hands and she takes a deep breath to keep from sobbing. she tries to keep her eyes closed, but she opens them at the worst moment: she saw fat guy holding a plastic bag with small piece of flesh coated with blood inside. he tossed it into a huge plastic bin labeled "hazardous waste." And while she sat in the "recuperating room," suffering from perhaps the most

dizzying cramps in the universe, she still held on to that one statement. and even if the fat guy rampaged her insides, even if the manipulative boyfriend took most of her heart & soul, her mind was still there, still hers, and she held onto it, fiercely. by making sure she herself realized something throughout all of this, that even though she knew that this was the right thing to do at this time and age, she continued to think:

Nunca pense que yo terminaría así - *

Irma Román

* - i never thought i'd turn out like this

Why Women Wear High Heels

Why Women Wear High Heels?

Because we want to look tall,

being so short

and we want to feel good,

feeling so sad

Why Women Wear High Heels?

Because we hate ourselves?
Or maybe love ourselves
or we want to look pretty
being unattractive

Why Women Wear High Heels?

Because you don't have to be rich
to wear high heels
you can be very poor
you can also be fat
or skinny or just a medium size

Why Women Wear High Heels?

Who invented them anyway?
It was a man who hated his wife,
his mother, and his sister
because they were mean to him
when he was growing up
one day he decided to invent

a new way of torture
And punish all women
for life and centuries to come
He formed a secret society
and all men belong to it
for hundreds of years
they've been meeting
all over the world
to plan new ways of torture
to destroy female feet
to unbalance our bodies
and create varicose veins
in our legs

Why Women Wear High Heels?

Because we love them
you can see high heels
in small towns, in big
and small cities, on farms,
women wear high heels
to go to church,
to dance, to go to work,
to look for employment,
to file for unemployment
to see lawyers or doctors
to enter or get out of
the hospitals
women wear high heels
on dirt or marble floors
on carpeted or wood floors
on roads full of stones in Latin America
women wear high heels

EVERYWHERE
we wear high heels
to parties, to lunches, to dates,
to get married, to file for divorce,
to attend birthday parties
or to go to a funeral
to drive cars, to ride buses,
fly in airplanes,
bicycles and motorcycles

Why Women Wear High Heels?

Sometimes two inches, four,
six or even eight inches high
many women have lost
their balance
and have fallen on the ground
walking in those heels
serious consequences
have occurred
broken ankles
pulled muscles
bloody knees
but we keep wearing
those high heels

Why Women Wear High Heels?

SISTERS - STOP! STOP!
Punishing ourselves
STOP the pain in our tired feet
Let's start a REVOLUTION
a feet REVOLUTION
STOP! STOP!
RIGHT NOW!

PLEASE STOP!
Wearing high heels
Let's all go BAREFOOT!

Daisy Cubias

At a Party in the Dark Halls with my Sister of the Night

With raven hair and a beauty of her own
I follow her into my worst fear
with a trembling heart and bowed head
I step forward on the chill stone path

There under torchlit halls
I see my own true self
There in the presence of those I have fought with
I seek the knowledge of power and place

I saw dark amused faces
(I killed his brothers in battle I believe)
I hear harsh laughter
(Did I wound him by the gates?)

I sense my sister at my side
Unknown to these demons in this dank hall
Our father watches our friendship warily
he doesn't know we know yet

I raise my chin
I will swear to no one to whom I swear my fidelity
I flung my own dark hair down my back
I am who I am

With pride, I stand next to my sister
and still my heart from the chill

We are found
and none can drive us apart

Lucy Román

The Journey Home

today, i awake, with a restlessness of spirit,
something stirring inside,

i have been thinking lately of quality of life, of
    going beyond merely living,
of life pulsing through every cell every second,
have i lost my fire, my passion,
does it disappear with too much pain, too much
    hardship

the sun is shining and i bask in it, wash my spirit in
    its radiance,
and my hands yearn,
to enter rich, moist earth,
she is waking, she is waking…as am i…
called to emergence by the voice of thunderbeings,
echoing through my many-chambered heart…held
    on the breath of wind

and i have seen their streak of light, premonition in
    southern sky,
and i have heard their ancient text long before
    church bells rang,
and i have been touched by their rain,
carving the map of my life, their life, lest i forget, in
    my chicana face,
tattooing my spirit with migrations; quetzalcoatl, la
    llorona,
weaving into fiber of muscle the knowledge of
    sowing and harvesting,
tending the maize,

planting on the tip of my tongue songs to summon
     the rain gods for my sister maize is very thirsty
and filling my belly with rhythms of grinding,
     matate, bone against bone

i have seen the world birthed anew with each rising
     sun
and the red skies of dusk as the sacrificed mothers
     bring her to rest and i look closely,
for my own, who gave up her spirit long ago,
as day becomes night, and grandmother shows her
     face and it is full,
and spirits of the night rise from their sleep, like
     tendrils of smoke, coil and wrap around trees,
slither under doorways, mists under yellow street
     lamps, they inhabit the night,
a tongue searching narrow alley, calling us into
     sleep,
mija, mija it is time
your aunty is waiting,
and i am at the threshold, space between life and
     death,
i crawl, answering ancient instinct, hands and feet
     mold into imprints left long ago,
i crawl upon earth, into womb, and there i am
     embraced

and today i awake with a restlessness of spirit and
     something is stirring within,
calling me, to what? where? and i do not know,
so i make this mark,
on this page,
attempt to mold my experience with words,

give testimony to a circle of elders that do not exist,
feed the sacred fire that burns in my chest,
longing to lay my rawness upon fertile earth,
but out this double-pained window all i see is
	concrete, weighing heavy,
upon the breast of our mother,
i wonder if she can draw breathe into her lungs or
	have her ribs collapsed,
under the weight of man's stupidity and arrogance,
i look out, this time through my pained lenses and i
	see strips of her brown skin,
guarded by winding, twisted roots of warrior trees
	claiming this space as their own,
today i will weave a cocoon around my rawness,
	plant the seed of transformation in my belly,
feed possibility as i wrap silk fibers through my
	hair, anoint my skin with the oil of my dreams,
feed my life on the bone and blood meal of my
	ancestors,
and i will tease the stirrings within, until they are a
	deafening roar…pulsating, breathing,
pushing against crusted earth, begging for release,
and where they rest, awaiting germination, it is
	deep, dark, and they are alone, as am i,
and in the wake of their emergence,
i am

Debra Barrera Pontillo

The Sisterhood of Woman of Color

(A tribute to us)

The dishes are done. My report to the President of the company is ready. My son is not going to kill himself because life is not fair and my daughter has promised not to shave her head again. Another normal day sets in the sunset.

Finally Calgon takes me away. Not to an island, but through those paths I have been walking with women of color. Women who are mother earth, but also storms and thunder. Women who carry their culture, not in their sleeves, but in their heads and their bodies. Women whose lives were shattered many times, but always got new mirrors.

I've walked those paths with Irma, a Chicana. Her strength tempered by her love, her commitment. The Aztec spirits shaped her soul and gave her the wisdom of an old "curandera," a healer. She has been with me even when I was not with me.

And then there is Helen, a Black woman, with the dignity of an Old World chief. Her words travel clear, like a natural spring, because they are honest. Her eyes see what is there and what needs to be there. Her heart quietly, without imagery or trepidation, projects love and friendship to those she welcomes into her life.

There are so many Brown, Black, Native American, and Asian women who have touched and continue to touch my life. Anita proud, brown woman and her daughters, each living by their own interpretation of what a mujer is. And there is Tish, so caring it hurts her. Her heart

goes in all directions and sometimes it swells to allow for troubled children, confused mothers, runaway minds and souls trying to find a place they trust, a place to rest. And there is Dorothy a Stockbridge Munsie, projecting, by her words and actions, the values put in her hands by her ancestors. And Agnes, Filipina, who without knowing, taught me important lessons.

We all live, love, hurt, survive and conquer. Our struggles vary but our tools are similar: our inner strength, our love for our men, our children, our elders, our self-respect and sense of history. The knowing who we were, who we are and what's important.

So I salute you, women of color. I salute you sisters in life. I toast for what you did, and what you are doing. But most important, I toast to what we will be and what we will be doing.

Gladis Benavides

In Between the Doorway

My eyes see the people around me.
Climbing high the corporate ladder,
So much pushing and shoving goes on
in between steps.
Some have fallen down and met me, eye to eye.

I admit there are times that I contemplate wearing
the hose,
the heels,
the navy blue skirt suit.
I fantasize walking with a briefcase in hand.
My neck stretched up like a giraffe.
I impress people with intelligence.

Yet my heart is a mom's heart.
The heart that stays at home.
The heart that gives of herself.
The heart that lives with sesame street.
That wakes up many nights attending asthma
        attacks!

No time for pantyhose.
Highheels.
And briefcase in hand.
At least I have not fallen!

Margarita Dumit

In the Wavering Light

She sat before me
an alabaster statue
Her eyes mirror my own
in the flickering candlelight
She called me sister

A memory of loving arms
a bright flash of light during my lonely childhood
a moment suspended in time

I had clutched at her skirts
I hid behind her and her name
unknowingly my oldest sibling
Unaware
she had even then been there for me

In a court of suspicions and deceit
She was the one I feared
and thought the world of.
The one I had wished to be
When I grow up

Now
in another life time
we sit across from each other
Seeing for the first time
that which others have always seen
sisters

Lucy Román

Gigi and I

It's a beautiful day
when my daughter and I
sit down together...

Our womanness expressed
in individual and personal ways.
Our spirits ripened with
the sun of different springs.

It's a beautiful day
when my daughter and I
sit down together...

Comparing notes gathered
in different notebooks.
Looking at each other
with the eyes of the heart.
Listening to each other...
quietly, no interruptions.

It's a beautiful day
when my daughter and I
sit down together...

It's as if she and I
met in the crossroads
and found a new road
to walk together.

It's a beautiful day
when my daughter and I
sit down together...

Gladis Benavides

Virgins, am I the first and who's better????

Women
Admit you're not a virgin!
Whore!
Say that you are, and…
Why did you do it with me?
Say you have been with his friend, and…
Am I bigger, better, best?
Say he's as bad as the REST!?!

Rosa Salinas-Hultman

The Sacred Space of Emptiness

the sacred space of emptiness...
what is this thing that hungers so in the
depths of my spirit... ravaging my soul....
unfulfilled loss... mourn my days and
sing to the nights... a wailing song... hollow...
my lament to all children lost...in the shuffle
to survive... no pattern on the floor...
step, ball change, step... only the abyss...
patiently waiting...
this surface is the landscape of my body...
and here over my heart lies
this sacred space of emptiness...
reach in through flesh, through bone
and touch this beating heart and feel the moistness,
of blood, drop down and out...
spread myself over earth; a fertile offering,
dark red into black...
if only... if only...

a mother's love found its way,
into this little life, little girl, hungers
searching the night, not knowing what for,
or what drives her
her fingers picking at the rotting flesh
around the edges of
this sacred space of emptiness

night bird flies, swooping down to partake
in the feast, on the edge of a life,
spun tightly as she danced in the warm,
dark fluid world of womb,

soon nightbird hears a soft, crackling voice,
startled, nightbird pauses, and the voice whispers
i am here nightbird, here in this sacred space
of emptiness,
do not eat from my rotting flesh,
for it causes me pain,
and i am just a little girl
but if you bury me deep in the earth for the night
so no other animal eats my rotting flesh
then when i awake from the womb of the earth,
i will forever sing to the nightbirds in the evening
sky

Debra Barrera Pontillo

Mamá's Prayer

Lately, I don't see her much.
But I always dream of her.
Mamá is always on my mind.

She is praying for me,
I know.

From the time she gets up,
To the time she goes to bed,
For the past fourteen years,
Since I left home,
Mamá worries.

She is praying for me,
I know.

She calls me on Saturdays
Before she goes to church.
Her call is to remind me that I should do the same.
"If you go to church on Saturday," she says,
"You don't have to go on Sunday."

She is praying for me,
I know.

Mamá goes to church on Saturday,
In case she cannot go on Sunday.
But she always goes on Sundays anyway.

She goes to church every day.
From Monday to Friday, at seven a.m.

She and dad are always there.

She is praying for me,
I know.

Mamá calls me on Sundays
To make sure I went to church.
Almost always
I tell her I go even though I really don't.
I can imagine the pain in her if I say the truth.

When I do,
        tears in silence run down
the wrinkles of her aging face.
She hurts!

She prays for me.

Fourteen years!
I think by now she knows, but doesn't say a thing.
Probably thinks I have gone stray.
But, she does not tell me to my face.

She prays instead.

Alfonso Zepeda-Capistrán

The Translation

He shot her because she told him to. That was his answer whenever anyone who visited him at the Malheur County Jail tried to make sense of his nonsense. His court appointed lawyer was about to attempt to interview him again. Burt Hutchins had been to the jail earlier that day but the little Spanish he picked up on vacations to Manzanillo didn't help. Burt was 62, had a general practice like all other nine lawyers in the county. Never done a shooting before. Not many shootings come up in this place. That being the case, Burt was as able as anyone to defend the man. Burt had heard the guy confess anyway. They got him on tape.

The second time Burt showed up with an interpreter. Not a trained translator, mind you, but an intake worker from downstairs in social services, Teodoro Muñoz. Other workers around the courthouse called him the Spanish guy to be polite as if being Mexican required a euphemism. Burt met the interpreter minutes ago in front of the jail's reception window.

"It's hard for me to say Teo-doro," the lawyer began,, spacing out the syllables in a way that sounded like *tío de oro,* the golden uncle. 'Mind if I call you Teddy?" Burt asked permission, wanting to set a casual tone with the interpreter.

Teodoro considered Burt Hutchins, an imposing man with good posture. He stood straight up at six feet tall. A mop of gray hair flopped atop of his head. Teodoro's eyes caught on the sterling silver scales of justice on the lawyer's lapel. Teodoro was a family man, the father of six boys. He wanted to cooperate with the lawyer but thought that there is a fine line between civility and agreeing to be put in your place. So he said politely, "Mr. Hutchins, I prefer that you call me Tito." He was not about to let this hot shot in a pin-stripe suit and a bolo tie get cuddly with him.

"Tito it is," Burt extended his right hand and the two men shook hands. "Let's see what he's got," Burt said as he walked toward the door with the letters ATTORNEY printed on its glass window. The two entered the cramped four-by-four-foot booth. Max was waiting for them, seated on the other side of a concrete wall that reached to about chest-high. From there a metal mesh grid that climbed all the way to the ceiling was all that separated inmate from freedom.

Burt said to Tito, "You translate my questions and then tell me what he says." Before Burt started his interview, though, Max wanted to make one thing clear.

"Dile que no me oriné, pero que en este cuarto huele hasta mierda." Tito explained what Max said to Burt: that the stench of urine and defecation in that small room was not of Max's making.

"Don't worry about it," Burt reassured Max, "it's an old jailhouse. I've seen and smelled worse." Burt wanted to get to the motive for the shooting. Why did he do it?

"She said she wanted to die. Said shoot me, shoot me," Max told the two from the other side of the screen. "That's why."

"Yes," Burt wasn't alarmed yet, "she may have said that after she saw you pointing at her, but why did you take the gun out in the first place?"

"Ella me obligó."

"He says she made him do it," Tito explained.

"What do you mean, she forced you to shoot her?" Burt looked Max squarely in the eye with his question.

"I had no choice,"

"Tell him to cut the crap," Burt instructed Tito. He was starting to show impatience with Max. Tito told Max "to get serious."

"She didn't make you do it. She wasn't the one who handed you the gun." Burt pressed.

"No, not like that." Burt couldn't believe the lawyer this time.

"Then how?"

"She provoked me when she called me *mada faca.*"

"What'd he say about the cow?" Burt was anxious for Tito to explain that one.

"I said *mada faca, not mada vaca.*" Max corrected the lawyer himself.

"Mada what?"

"Dile que la pinche vieja me rayó la madre." Max

raised his voice to almost a shout. He asked Tito to tell his lawyer that the woman had profaned his mother.

Like others in town Tito knew of the woman, though he didn't know her. For that reason, Tito tried to clarify the question before translating for Burt.

"That's what she said to you?" Tito asked Max in a tone of disbelief.

"Just like that," Max pounded his fist on his side of the counter. Tito still didn't believe him.

"She speaks mainly English," Tito reminded Max about *la vieja*. "Almost never talks in Spanish."

Tito was right. She was known to claim that she spoke only a word here and there of Spanish. Those who lived on the East side of the underpass called her type *agringada* because she tried to be something she wasn't. West of the underpass she stood out like a stubborn coffee stain on white enamel. She was more assimilated than she had a right to be. She had nothing to show for it.

Max insisted: *"Te digo que la vieja me mandó a chingar la madre. I tell you she called me a mada faca."* He said. "I may not understand English well, but I know that when a *gringo* calls you a *mada faca*, it means *chinga tu madre."*

"Ah, *sí, sí, sí,"* Tito nodded his head with understanding and turned to Burt to start to explain. *"Mada faca* is Max's way of pronouncing mother fucker. She provoked him," Tito pointed at Max with his thumb, "calling him a mother fucker. That means *chinga tu madre.* And, Mr. Hutchins," Tito hemmed a little, "that's...well, let's just say she drew the first blood."

Burt turned his attention away from Tito and to his client on the other side of the screen.

"That's it? That's your reason? All because she called you a mother fucker?"

"Seguro, " Max was adamant. "Of course. A man can't stand by with his arms crossed when someone has mentioned his mother in that vulgar way."

Burt listened intently, if disappointed that so far he had nothing to work with.

"Not me. No sir." Max went on. "I don't take that from anyone. *Y cuando es una vieja, menos. "*

"He says," Tito translated, "that he wouldn't take that from a man, much less from a woman."

"No es que mi madre fuera una santa, " Max still explained. "It's not that his mother is some saint," Tito translated. "But when she mentions my mother in that way, that's the worst insult to me," Max thumped at his breastbone with two fingers to show that his umbrage ran deep. "If I don't do something about it," Max continued, "I might as well join the circus."

Burt did not understand that at all and hoped that it was because of a faulty translation. "What'd he say about the circus?" Burt turned to Tito for help.

Tito understood perfectly and tried again to explain it to Burt. "He means that a man can't allow himself to be insulted," Tito first spoke slowly because he wasn't sure how to put what was coming delicately, then said the rest of the sentence real fast, "with words of his mother being laid." Glad to be done with that, Tito resumed his normal pace of talking. "That kind of talk, Mr. Hutchins, uh-uh," Burt lowered his head and swung it slowly from side to side to indicate that a man can't allow it. "That kind of talk from a woman," Tito repeated, "takes away everything that makes a man a man. It's not done." Burt only stared back blankly with no sign of understanding. Tito thought that for all the education this lawyer had, he sure was being dense.

Next Tito tried to explain with gestures. He made a knife-slicing motion with his hand as he said, "It's like having been castrated." Still Tito saw no sign of recognition from Burt. "So a man might as well join a freak show," Tito added and paused, "…as a eunuch."

"Oh," Burt grimaced and shifted his stance a little as if he felt the pain of Tito's castrating gesture, "it's that bad."

"Now you see," Max tilted his head to the lawyer who finally seemed to get the point.

"Tell him," Burt said to Tito, "that kind of provocation won't be enough. Got to have more than words."

"But they're not just words," Max interrupted before Tito had a chance to translate. "When she said *mada faca,* I had to make her pay."

"I know what you're saying," Burt tried to show sympathy, "but it's not going to work."

The look in Max's eyes alone questioned the lawyer's response. *"¿Cómo que no?* What does he mean, it won't work. What kind of a lawyer did they give me here? *Un guaje."* So far, Max thought, the lawyer had shown the spine of a ripe banana. But Burt would have the final word.

"Tell him, Tito," Burt put his right hand up for emphasis and enunciated the words simple, slow, and deliberate: "There's no such thing as a mother fucker defense."

Teresa Elguézabal

The First Time

you tell your father "I love you."
is not easy. For we are taught
to love women .... not men.
My father was the one I wanted
to be near, to feel his strength,
to know his passion for life.
The distance between us went unnoticed
until that fateful day - the phone call.
It would be my first airplane ride
from Cincinnati to Detroit,
ironically, to be with him at death.
Funny, for years I saved the ticket stub
not sure whether to remind me
of my first flight or his death.

Standing next to him,
I remember being
strong - after all, I was his namesake
and others were expecting me
to be a man.

The day I cried was months later,
when I went to my mailbox
for his weekly letters and poems.
The box was empty - no letter, no poems.

I was so alone. Lost. Confused.
I had been taught about sex,
but no one had explained
the overwhelming sensations
that arrive with the death

of the man who for twenty years,
I called "papa."

He lay so still, properly embalmed.
His amigos from the Monterrey Poolroom
paid their final respects.
The priest said some stupid prayers.
I cursed God for the strange feel ng
of being a young man without a father.
I wanted to hug him one last time
or would it be our first?
The line from the poem he wrote to me,
after my leaving home,

> "it was papa who took a drink
> and wanted to hug you tight"

floated around
like a bad taste in my mouth.

Now the distance between the family
has separated us to different parts of the country.
Mama lost her voice,
she quietly waits for your return
at the Nightingale Nursing Home.
She teaches us a lesson - how sometimes
death sneaks slowly up on you
weakens you till your last breath.
Now, I struggle to be father
for my beautiful ten-year-old daughter.
You are not here but I want you to know
I don't blame you anymore.

The poet in me wants to share a poem
with you, make you smile, laugh
but all I can do is tell the children
"... my father was a poet."
I feel so proud, at the precise moment
when I express your words with my voice:
but I remember too well
how the first time I told my father
"I love you"... was not easy.

Trinidad Sánchez, Jr.

María Eugenia Ruíz de Medina

Mi madre sufre porque padre volvió a casa.
Mi madre sufre porque los hijos ya son grandes.
Mi madre sufre porque una hija está enamorada.
Mi madre sufre porque el hijo fuma marijuana.
Mi madre sufre porque la hija se fue de casa sin
      estar casada.
Mi madre sufre porque las vecinas hablan mal de
      ella.
Mi madre sufre cada vez que el hijo vocifera "usted
      es un hijo de puta."
Mi madre sufre cuando piensa en los Estados
      Unidos.
Mi madre sufre cuando se levanta y escucha a los
      pájaros.
Mi madre sufre aunque conoce la rabia.
Mi madre sufre porque lava ropa ajena.
Mi madre sufre porque la hija organiza obreros.
Mi madre sufre porque la hija puede ser
      secuestrada.
Mi madre sufre cuando va al mercado y platica con
      los comerciantes.
Mi madre sufre cuando recibe cartas de sus hijos.
Mi madre sufre porque el dinero ya no le alcanza.
Mi madre sufre porque la hija es importante.
Mi madre sufre porque alguien murió en el barrio.
Mi madre sufre porque conoce su edad.
Mi madre sufre cuando la elegancia abre la boca.
Mi madre sufre cuando hay silencio.
Mi madre sufre cuando suenan las campanas de la
      iglesia.
Mi madre sufre cuando los niños sueñan.

Mi madre sufre porque la hija está de nuevo
    embarazada.
Mi madre sufre en los días de fiesta.
Mi madre sufre porque la hija está desempleada
    después de 17 años de escuela.
Mi madre sufre porque la hija fue despedida del
    trabajo.
Mi madre sufre porque la hija se defendió del
    patrón.
Mi madre sufre porque el hijo es artista.
Mi madre sufre porque el hijo sufre.
Mi madre sufre cuando escucha a Pérez Prado.
Mi madre sufre cuando llueve.
Mi madre sufre porque conoce este poema.
Mi madre sufre cuando sonríe,
Ustedes ya sufren porque conocen a mi madre.
    Etcétera.

A Ricardo Medina

Rubén Medina

My Father was a Macho...and I loved him

My father was a gentle man. His mestizo face lovingly carved by joys, sorrows and warm, sunny rays. His greenish, grayish eyes always squinting, like lips with half smiles.

I remember watching him when I was a child, as he sat in the backyard with his mind, spirit and body in quiet harmony. He was a man of sayings: "it all comes out in the mirror" or "words are like oil." My favorite has become my definition for coalitions: "juntos pero no revueltos." It means, together but not scrambled.

When he talked to us, my brother, my sister and me, he spoke about truth, integrity and love. He did sit at the head of the table and demanded our deference. He loved and treated my mother as a partner, a lover, a mother and a wife. You see, my father was a macho and I loved him. Machismo, in my cultural dictionary is hombria, manhood -- a macho is the oiled, tan, muscular guy with a woman hanging from his left shoulder in a shaving cream commercial. He is not the woman hater or the wife beater. He is not the enemy in the battle of the sexes, or the tough man with a distorted view of his manhood. He is who he is and not who he is made to be. So machismo is okay with me, because you see, my father was a macho and I loved him.

Gladis Benavides

163

Democracy

it was decided by the noisier of the people who are
delegated such powers by those who just don't give
a damn that America was not such a bad place after
all it being july and who needs heat or hot water in
this weather anyway and at night when everyone is
out the tenements don't look quite so bad and who
sees them in the daytime when everyone is sleeping
away the heat and the war was good for the
economy reducing unemployment by sending the
men to war and creating jobs for the women who
could work for the guys who did not go to war and
who were making big bucks and the underground
economy was providing enough luxury items to go
round and so it was decided by the noisier of the
people who are delegated such powers by those who
just don't give a damn that America was not such a
bad place after all to celebrate by doing what would
have been done anyway as it had become a tradition
for the fourth of July so each side sent out its scouts
to Chinatown and little Italy to gather up as much
firepower as could be bought or stolen and to
smuggle it and stockpile it and to distribute it at just
the right time which was sunset on the fourth of july
when it was decided by the noisier of the people
who are delegated such powers by those who just
don't give a damn that America was not such a bad
place after all to celebrate by doing what would
have been done anyway as it had become a tradition
and so the two armies of teenagers too young for
draftcards or too mean by means of their criminal
records for military service assumed positions on

their respective

 rooftops the ruddy Irish above their red bricked
tenements and the swarthy, Puerto Ricans and
leftover Italians above their brown bricked
tenements and it was decided by the noisier of the
people who are delegated such powers by those who
just don't give a damn that America was not such a
bad place after all to celebrate by doing what would
have been done anyway as it had become a tradition
that the war at home had begun which was signaled
by a single rocket's red glare which began the
shooting of bottle rockets and m-80's and strings of
firecrackers and sizzlers which went on for hour
after hour keeping the old ladies and babies awake
and driving the dogs crazy they cowered in corners
like shell-shocked veterans though casualties were
light as the street was wide and nothing more than a
sputtering rocket ever hit the other side mostly
everything landed in the street which was by mutual
decision a free-fire zone and anyone or anything in
it an enemy to both sides and mostly there was no
one in it except a few unfortunate passersby
unaware of this great fourth of july tradition and a
line of parked cars which would be pockmarked by
morning when the sidewalks were covered with red
white and blue paper and the air reeked of sulfur
and it was decided that everyone should ceasefire
and get some chow and shuteye and rest up for the
night when it was decided by the noisier of the
people who are delegated such powers by those who
just don't give a damn that America was not such a
bad place after all to celebrate by doing what would
have been done anyway as it had become a tradition

and the sun went up and down on the ceasefire and
the Irish and the Puerto Ricans and the leftover
Italian guys and their girls and their mothers and
fathers and sisters and brothers got back out on our
street to hang out to rock babies to gamble to play
loud music to drink to gossip to party and to wait to
wait to wait for a job for a baby for a draft notice
which had become a tradition in not such a bad
place after all

wr rodriguez

Value

Images given by the words.
Hands that are used to work.
Roads that are endless...
Ambition that draws our vision...
Neither history nor art are part of time.
Coins aren't owned by a race.
They have less value than plastic.

Sunglasses doesn 't mean that he is blind.
Alike the minds that see images rather than souls.
Paralytic conscious of all ages can be-reconstructed
        before it flows among different nations
        who end up being our neighbors.

A humanitarian doesn't want money.

A humanitarian teaches the value-of-deception.

Rafael Gómez

Take the South out of South Africa

I'm gonna take the South out of South Africa
the home of the slaves
and the land of no freedom

I'm gonna take the South out of South Africa
where George Wallace stood
on the university steps
and said no blacks
no blacks shall enter here
except over my dead
and crippled body.

I'm gonna take the South out of South Africa
where separate but equal means
that blacks lived in the homelands
and not in their homes

I'm gonna take the South out of South Africa
where Jim Crow laws
have tried to change the colors
but it's still the same old shackles
called Apartheid

I'm gonna take the South out of South Africa
where young people are detained
without trials/without lawyers/ without rights
but never without hope

I'm gonna take the South out of South Africa

Oscar Mireles

Crónica Chicalanga

Abandonaron
la ciudad de sus dioses
en el siglo siete
de la era cristiana
según se viene llamando
tentativamente.

Es todavía un misterio
la causa de la partida.
Las malas lenguas
hablan de sacrificios
al ciclo de Venus,
guerras secretas,
enfermedades extrañas.

Algunos regresaron al oriente
a seguir tallando piedras enormes,
colosales.

Otros buscaron
planicies verdes donde erigir de nuevo sus templos.
Otros caminaron al norte
y pronto se establecieron
en la orrillas de lagunas de agua salada y aves
rosadas donde habitaban hombres arrogantes
y extraños hábitos
que también veneraban al sol.

Vinieron lluvias, cometas, truenos.
En el Valle floreció una ciudad jamás soñada.
El sol y la luna permanecían

durante el día en ambos lados del cielo.
Volvió a nacer la astrología,
los privilegios,
los dioses insaciables.

Hombres nunca vistos
con pelos en el rostro
empezaron a merodear por esos rumbos.
Pronto terminaron imponiendo
un dios igualmente cruel,
sin máscara.

La tierra dejó de ser
un gran útero.
Se convirtió en mina,
propiedad de un solo hombre.

Degollamientos, destrucción de palacios
y libros sagrados, espejos quebrados, peste.
Las piedras fueron vueltas a tallar.

Con la nueva aparición del cometa Haley
volvieron a emprender el viaje
al norte.

Tepiteños, tlatelolcas, iztapalapeños,
tlaneplantas, mixcoacenses, tetepanos,
tlalpaleños, xochimilcas, coyoaquenses,
tacubeños, cuitlahuenses, nativitas,

En estos días
muchos ya se nombran
Chicalangos.

Y por aquí andan
casi indistingibles
a lado de los sonoras, totonacos, coahuilenses,
durangueños, michoacanos, sinaloenses, zapotecos,
erigiendo una nueva nación,
un nuevo milenio.

Rubén Medina

Comfortably Non-political
(Santafé de Bogotá, D. C.)

The aluminum bird
and
its electronic equipment
lift me soaring
above the
smoking sea
of brick
violence
industry
garbage
poverty
and
pollution
in which
the Bogota savannah
drowns
and
my heart
trembles
as it anticipates
the chilly academic chatter
that
will fly with me
from Chicago
to Madison
wrapping me in ice
floating in
      its airs
      its conceits
      its indifference

                    smiling
                              and comfortably
                                        non-political.

Rino Avellaneda

Cómodo Apolitismo
(Santafé de Bogotá, D. C.)

El pájaro de aluminio
y su
equipo electrónico
me elevan
sobre el
humenate mar
de ladrillo
violencia
industria
basura
pobreza
y contaminación
en que se asfixia
la Sabana de Bogotá
y
mi corazón
tiembla
al anticipar
la gélida cháchara académica
que
conmigo volará
de Chicago
a Madison
abrigándome en hielo
    flotando en
        sus aires
        sus humos
        sus indiferencias
            y

su cómodo apolitismo.

Rino Avellaneda.

Tijuana Border

E1 camino al sur
eventualmente
te lleva a una ciudad enorme
construida sobre la tragedia
--es el trueno.

Hacia el norte,
con algo de suerte,
después de dos noches
de alucinación
y orden y uniformes
llegarías a San Pinche,
desierto para los ancianos
y parque de diversión
para algunos niños
--es el viento.

Hacia el este
solo existe
profesión de náufrago
o fotógrafo de kiosco,
hay sabiduría en ambas.
--es el agua.

Hacia el oeste
no hay destino fijo,
tienes que caminar
backwards,
de cara al sol,
puede ser
que algunos lean

los símbolos
en tus ojos.
--es el fuego.

Siempre puedes volver
a esta ciudad de paso,
ser un poeta sedentario.

Tu excentricidad
a final del siglo
sigue siendo
excentricidad
pero aquí
todos los caminos
cruzan,
todos los caminos
desembocan.
El trueno, el viento, el
agua, el fuego.

Rubén Medina

The Train

For Joe and Lori Bravo, With apologies to Clebo

The train ran through my poem,
ran straight through my poem.
I spoke louder and louder
but the train ran, ran, drove itself
right through my poem!
I said to my best friend
in the back of the room, I said:
Go throw yourself on the tracks!
I was serious. He laughed out loud.
the audience mistook this line
as part of the poem, but I was serious.
I'm serious about my poems.

The train drove itself through my poem
moments before the verse...

       ...and somewhere off in the distance a
       million women dressed like clowns
       were making love, faking orgasms to a
       million men.
       Neither of them was laughing ...
       the clowns were without eyes.
       They shuddered for the negative.

       Beauty is on the inside. How could they
       see it!
       The mariachi music in the foreground
       was the type
       my grandfather always listened to
       when he felt sad.

Once again with the sound of the train
off in the distance I raised my voice
and said to the stranger in the back,
he was no longer my friend.
I said: *Go throw yourself on the tracks.*
I never wanted another train
driving itself through my poem.
I was serious. He thought I was joking.
I'm serious about my poems.

Looking up from my notes
and the train having driven itself
through the center of my poem,
it was quite clear: this existential
moment was lost...
The audience had missed
the whole meaning of the poem.

Trinidad Sánchez, Jr.

Rain

A week of rain.
A week of dark, sunless skies.
A cooling of the earth.

The windows in my home were left open
Inviting the rain-cool breeze
To share my summer's sleep.

There was rhythm in the air.
Wet beads bouncing off leaves,
Hitting my gutters as if they were empty drums.
Rain was dancing on my roof
and splashing in its own
Pools on cloud-mirrored sidewalks.

It was a week of rain.
A week of cool summer kisses.
It was a week waiting for poetry.

Pedro Villarreal

Uninspired

it's late
i have no ideas to share with you
i don't have anything smart or artistic to say
i don't have any emotions to gush out for you

all i've been doing lately
is giving people the blank stare nowadays

i don't care to voice
any opinions
about the death of my ancestors

i don't feel anything
for the friends who've
died over the past ten years

I feel indifferent to the
past and future lovers
that will enter my life

i could care less if i die tonight

just as long as you know:
that i've existed in this boring world
and i'm sorry that when you asked me for
something straight from my heart

and all i handed you was this insensitive crap.

Irma Román

My Poetry

They are too short, I have been told.
Not enough words.

There are more beads
In a rosary. There are
More notes in a blue jay's song.

Not enough thought, or shape or style.
Why don't they rhyme? Is that all there is?

I offer no one the promise of a feast.
If I bring you berries, then eat!

I offer no one
A full-length mirror of thought.
I prefer shards on strings.

My poetry is not about words.
It is about breathing.

When that same old day
Has its arms wrapped around my neck,
When darkness begins to appear,
When I can no longer breathe out,

It is a poem that breaks the hold
And fills my lungs with oxygen.
My poetry gives me life,
Not my words.

Pedro Villarreal

Rafael Marrero

Sold out my pueblo
With his racist "El Pito"
Se cree crítico
Of my Gente
Says it's wrong to be independiente
Fat Colorado con la grande Frente

You criticize my friends
Like José López and Luis Guttierez
And then you criticize mi mújer
Solo para ser
Una que píensa
¿Qué es bueno no ser vendida?
you call my land a colonization
trying to rob us like a hurricane of Haitians

You'd better stop disrespecting
because we're a nation
we're not a U.N. creation
or a dump for U.S. Corporations
McOndo or Macondo?

Why question facts
our culture is getting attacked
by vende Patrias
So Borinqueños, get up strike back
¡Ahora!

Back to Plaza Carolina
We are not Americans hoes
Don't disrespect my women
They're not a commodity to be sold
just because they're pretty with skin of gold.

Trigueña is your skin
Latinas so fly. Where do I begin?
You must have wings you're so fly
I feel I'm on drugs looking in your eyes
yet you get abused
use for sterilization
they want us as tourist attractions
Like they "fucked" the Hawaiians

I'm Borinqueño and proud
once again, Puerto Rican, proud
Wanna know where my roots is?
Hato Rey, via Madison where I live Biz
Time for revolution, not spliffs
Representando unión, Paz
A Colectiva Y Mecha
Llaro Paz a BSU and anybody with a clue
No more Marreros,
Remember your Pueblo!

Enrique Fernández Roberts

JAPAN

Sucker I Exuma
Call me Yokozuma

I was in Nagasaki
Tokyo, Roppyngi
I saw the spot with the Bomb
America was wrong
More foul than a red card
Rough like mustard
The past is hard to swallow

We must be harder than Shingen in Nagoya
Strong like the castle in Kymamoto
Don't just wait for lotto
Or watch the tea brew
Stand up, polish your boots
We always wipe our feet before entering a room
Fukuora was a sweet
And instant gratification retreat
In the park, I drank Asahi Brew
Maybe a can or two
Erased my memory, I can't remember Japan

Can you?
Get less militant?
No puedo
Because
I miss Japan and Tsunamis
Nijon Shy, er I mean Sake
Asian women, Ramen
Sushi and Habachi

I rhyme like Fat Karaoke
A few cuban cigars got smokey

I saw a lush green land
A now miss a Borinqueño in Japan
I discovered myself
In the place I least expected
But better there than nowhere, I guess

Soon after civilized baths
Expensive bags
Metros and Mt. Aso in Osaka
I was stuck on a plane, got jet lag
Flew back on JAL not Asiana
So customs didn't check my bag of Marijuana

Now here it's cold
And I have no more mizo
To remind me of Nijon
Just a bottle of Sho chy
And I feel I'm gone.

Enrique Fernández Roberts

Yo Me Sigo

As I stand slightly outside of this immense sea of
Badger red
On the edge of some vast distant future
These questions constantly reemerge
Why have I abandoned chorizo and taco mornings,
Abuelos' scent of tres flores and cigarette,
Late night stops at Taco Cabana to dilute one too
many Bud Lights,
The sound of my mother yelling
"¡Levantate cabrón!"
Sure my father was reluctant to dar cariño but there
where moments when a hand shake meant
~I love you, Cuidate~,
why have I fled so alcanza
What happened to Valerio Longoria & Steve
Jordan's valses, redobas, y polkas
What fate yet awaits me
¿On tan mis raizes, my lengua, mi gente?
Have I stumbled on to a forsaken path
Will I stand to both mine and others expectations
Have I already failed?
No-me sigo, marchando: gritando
Leaping into the undetermined, into the unexplored
Carrying the threads of my ancestry, los recuerdos,
el futuro, y el espíritu de mi familia
To bind and weave them into a colorful tapestry so
that others might remember
The struggles and joys of the past
We must learn from each other and gain hope and
happiness from life's experiences cherish every
breath

Levantar nuestras voces in harmony and sing like
our ancestors sang
To birth and to death
We are all ONE,
juntos y humildes,
and together we shall return to the warm and
peaceful arms of our Mother Earth
So let the story unfold
There are no ends just new beginnings,
there are no ends just beginnings,
there are no ends just beginnings...

Nicolas Ramiro Valdéz

Mi Verano

Mi verano fue viaje del mundo
Carisimo fue el asunto
Para el oeste/avión 747
Estuve en Japón
Ví sus montañas
Admiré sus embras
Luego en Puerto Rico la playa
Allí sentado con barrilito y medalla
So now call me messaya
I have a message
Like a phophet
Followed, you
Were there, Hato Rey and Tokyo
Bailé al buen ritmo
Redescubrí cultura y ismaelo
Grito pa'que me oigan
Gente no me ignoren
Oral
No papel
Los blancos hablan solo miel
Dame lo que pido libertad
Pa' que sepan que el pueblo no se vendera
Escucha boricua
Resista la propaganda
Creada pro la raza blanca
Mentirosa
Son pro estadista
Soy independista
Se joda la politica
Represento la patria
Macondo poderes de majia

Ustedes mi familia
Como la mafia
Juntos seguiremos la marcha

Enrique Fernández Roberts